PRAYERS FOR DAILY LIFE

PRAYERS FOR DAILY LIFE

Ray Salmon

Copyright © 2011 Ray Salmon

The moral right of the author has been asserted.

Apart from any fair dealing for the purposes of research or private study, or criticism or review, as permitted under the Copyright, Designs and Patents Act 1988, this publication may only be reproduced, stored or transmitted, in any form or by any means, with the prior permission in writing of the publishers, or in the case of reprographic reproduction in accordance with the terms of licences issued by the Copyright Licensing Agency. Enquiries concerning reproduction outside those terms should be sent to the publishers.

Matador
5 Weir Road
Kibworth Beauchamp
Leicester LE8 0LQ, UK
Tel: (+44) 116 279 2299
Fax: (+44) 116 279 2277
Email: books@troubador.co.uk
Web: www.troubador.co.uk/matador

ISBN 978 1848765 320

British Library Cataloguing in Publication Data.
A catalogue record for this book is available from the British Library.

Typeset in 10.5pt Bembo by Troubador Publishing Ltd, Leicester, UK
Printed and bound in Great Britain by TJ International Ltd, Padstow, Cornwall

Matador is an imprint of Troubador Publishing Ltd

To all who pray.

PREFACE

I attended St. John's College, Durham, a college at that time primarily for men hoping to go into the ministry. For this reason students were encouraged to have a quiet time before morning chapel. The first prayer folder I have is dated July, 1956.

In the spring of 1961, following a brief prayer, I had an experience of the spirit. This experience I see as my conversion, and many things arose out of it, for example, since then I have believed that we live and move in an invisible, immaterial reality. Another was that I have started most weekdays with a quiet time. As my experience of the spirit had arisen out of a prayer, albeit brief, I felt the need to share the notion of prayer as a route to the divine for those wishing to take it. Unfortunately I lacked the nous of, say, a George Fox to create an effective ministry.

The years passed and in 1981 I took up the notion of having a writing period before going to work, the writing consisting of religious reflections and prayers. In the evening I drew and painted. Most of the prayers in this collection were written in this context, although since 2003 prayers have not been a part of my writing. Instead I have garnered any which have emerged in my quiet time. The ACTS approach to prayer explains their grouping since then: adoration, confession, thanksgiving and supplication, although the intercessions do not find a place.

The early prayers are patriarchal in tenor, but I have become gender inclusive over the years; also the divine is referred to as 'almighty', but given the freedom inherent in creation I now try to avoid this description.

The prayer books I have used in my quiet time include the following: Pelican Books' Daily Prayer, The Oxford Book of Prayer, Great Souls at Prayer and A Book of School Worship.

As with any prayer book we should feel free to adapt the prayers contained in this one to suit our particular outlook, preferences and circumstances.

THE PRAYERS

1. GOD LOVES STILL
Heavenly Father, please help me to love and to accept you as you are; and please help me to remember that in loving your children, I love you, their Father; and that in loving your creation, I love you, its Creator. Help me also to remember that when you turn a deaf ear to your child's requests, or indicate that a certain course is not to be pursued, that such responses are as much an expression of your love for your child as positive responses and opportunities. I recognise that you love your children, and know what is best for them in each situation. Heavenly Father, please help me to love you and to accept you as you are.

2. TO BE A CITIZEN!
Almighty God, please help me to live as a member of your kingdom today, and to point to you through my behaviour in what I think, say and do, and through my tasks, whether chosen or deputed. May your kingship alone be in the ascendant!

3. JUSTLY BEFORE GOD
Almighty God, help me to live today as a citizen of your kingdom, and to show forth justly through my behaviour and my tasks, chosen and deputed, the good things, the good qualities and the good gifts, which you bestow upon your citizens; that your name might be always recommended.

4. POINTING TO GOD
Almighty God, as a citizen of your kingdom help me to point to you through my behaviour, both by word and deed, and through my tasks,

whether chosen or assigned; that your kingship may be paramount and your name honoured.

5. PUT GOD FIRST

Almighty God, please help me at all times to put you first, to remember that my relationship to you is paramount: above my relationships within my family and at my place of work, above those where I worship, or at the club I attend. Let me remember always that you are my king, and that at all times I must try to behave in ways which honour you as my king. Your name alone be glorified!

6. WONDERFUL KING!

Almighty God, please help me to remember that my relationship to you is paramount, that at all times it takes pride of place in respect of the many relationships I enjoy, within the family and at my places of work and worship. Help me to put you first and to remember that you are my king, and as such must always be honoured by my words and my deeds. Wonderful King!

7. A GOOD SPIRIT

Almighty God, may our interior thinking and feeling be rational and reasonable, not strained unduly; may our outward conduct be rational and reasonable, be imbued with good-naturedness; and may the objectives we set ourselves and our modes of achieving them be rational and reasonable, accepting our limitations and situations as they are; that the work of your Good Spirit might go forward in a good spirit, and your Name be honoured and your will fulfilled.

8. FOR CLEANSING

Almighty God, when we close with you in worship and in prayer, we see ourselves as we are revealed by the light of your most Holy Spirit. Of your mercy, release us from the darkness which inhabits our souls, taking-up that place which is rightfully yours, only yours. Praise be!

9. FOR CLEANSING FROM THAT WHICH IS DISPLEASING TO GOD
Lord God, cleanse us from all that is displeasing to You, and not only sweep our homes clean, but furnish them with your own good self, your very own presence, that we might become and be citizens of your heavenly kingdom; for your name's sake we ask it.

10. INSTRUMENTS OF GOD'S LOVE
Almighty God, we live in your love; may my neighbour also live in your love through me.

11. FOR AN INCREASE OF POSSIBILITIES
Almighty God, we live in your love. May I not diminish that love for my neighbour, but rather furnish its increase by the increase of the possibilities I bring to the situation we are in.

12. HIS INSTRUMENT
Almighty God, we live in your love. May I not diminish that love for my neighbour, but rather enable its increase by the positive contributions I can bring to our relationship.

13. CHANNELS OF GOD'S LOVE
Almighty God , we live in your love; help us to be channels of that love for our neighbours.

14. WE LOVE EVERYONE
Almighty God, you love all your children; help us also to love all your children, each and everyone.

15. ATOMIC LOVE!
Almighty God, we live in your love: use every atom of our beings to express that love.

16. CARE FOR THE SICK
Almighty God, we live in your love; fill us with that love that we may meet the needs of all your children, and especially the very sick.

17. LOVE LIKE GOD'S
Almighty God, we live in your love; help us to accord to our neighbours the worth that you accord to them.

18. GRACIOUS GOD
Heavenly Father, we live in your grace. Help us to be gracious to our neighbours.

19. PRAYER FOR AN EMERGENCY
Lord, I feel at the end of my tether, I do not know which way to turn. I know from past experience that you know the best way forward, the right line to take, the correct thing to do in any situation. Please speak to me now, please show me which way to turn. Please!

20. PRAYER FOR BLESSING
Almighty God, I humble myself before you ,and beseech you to pour down your most Holy Spirit upon my family and relatives, my friends and acquaintances, and myself. Come, Holy Spirit, and bless us each one according to your purposes and our needs, that your name may be honoured and your will done.

21. MOST INEFFABLE ONE!

Most Ineffable One! whose name is Wonderful,
At whose side we live,
Warm our inner beings, cleanse our inner beings,
By the company of your self, your very own self,
That being thus warmed, being thus cleansed,
We may live more appropriately to the privileged position we enjoy,
By the side of One whose name is Wonderful.
Most Ineffable One! Alleluia! Lord!

22. FOR NOT AGAINST

Almighty God, help us to be for the institutions in which we pursue the various facets of our lives, and help us to express our positive attitude in positive thought and action; that your name might be vindicated, not besmirched.

23. GOD IS LOVE

Almighty God, we thank you that your name is Love, that you love and care for everyone, that you see everyone as an individual, each with his own hopes and fears, each with his own needs. We thank you that you love each one of us. As well as being recipients of your love, please help us to be sharers of your love with all in our lives, all your children! Alleluia!

24. BY GENUINE INTERESTS LOVE!

Almighty God, I thank you heartily for responding to my prayer for the coming of your most holy spirit upon the hearts and minds of your children known to me, and in particular I thank you for awakening in my heart and mind the understanding that my chief concerns, my real interests, may express love for my neighbour, may be instruments of your love for all your children. As well as pointing to you, my activities may be a means to loving my neighbour, and I praise and thank you for the opportunity and privilege this will bring during the coming days. Praise be to you, O God.

25.   SERVICE!
Almighty God, we thank you that Jesus came as one who serves, teaching us that true greatness is to be found not in lording it over others, but in serving them in love.

26.   HEAVENLY BIRTH
Lord God, I thank you for the birth of my body and of my soul. I thank you for making provision for my body, for its protection and maintenance, the warm, comfortable house and the daily, nourishing food. I thank you too for the provision you make for my soul: for the penitence you awaken, and the amendment of life which may follow; and for the understanding you inspire, and the new-found purpose and energy which may follow this. Lord God, I thank and praise you for the birth of my body and of my soul!

27.   TO ESCHEW EVIL
LORD GOD, please help us to oppose evil, not with the weapons of evil, whatever justification we may think we have for their use, for we must forswear evil in every way and on every occasion, but rather with your weapons of love and light.

28.   THE WILL OF GOD!
Almighty God, please help me to co-operate in your will and work, and help me also to accept any suffering and pain which this co-operation may entail; that your name may be honoured.

29.   CHILDREN OF GOD!
Almighty God, help us to stand straight when faced with evil, keeping a hold on the dignity ascribed by you to us as your children.

30.   OUR TRUST IN THE BENIGNITY OF GOD
O God, maker of the universe, whose home it is, we recognise and

applaud and stand humbled before your vast ability, and thus humbled affirm our trust in your purposes, your loving keeping and your overall design for the children of so great, so wonderful a creation.

31. GREAT CREATOR!

Almighty God, we stand awed before the immensity of the universe, the vast stretch of galactic formations, the colossal dimensions, millions upon millions of light years, recognising that you are within yet greater than these, that notwithstanding their great reach they are the product of your planning, of your creativity; help us to trust you implicitly in your planning and personal dealings in relation to your children, and to know that one so great, who orders that which is so great, can manage things well for his children who are so small, so very small. Praise be to you, O Creator God!

32. KEEPING ABREAST

Almighty God, we thank and praise you for your dynamic constancy. Help us not to make a model of one moment of it, but rather to offer ourselves openly and fully to its ever reforming, its ever re-energising, self-giving.

33. CHANNELS OF BLESSING

Almighty God, pour down your blessing on all those for whom we pray. Help us to be channels of your blessing, and to this end to forgive all whom we believe to have wronged us, not forgetting ourselves.

34. SNAP!

Almighty God, we thank and praise you for your ever-changing constancy. Help us to respond energetically to your energy, creatively to your creativity, and intelligently to your light, that is, to say 'snap!' with our lives.

35. ENJOY THE CHANGING WORLD
Almighty God, we thank and praise you for your dynamic and changing world; help us to relate to it positively, with acceptance and rejoicing, rather than negatively, with hostility and resentment.

36. AMAZING OPPORTUNITIES
Almighty God, we thank and praise you for the many and various opportunities which your changing world bestows upon us; help us to utilise these, rather than withdraw into sloth, for the benefit of our neighbours and ourselves; that your name may be honoured, and your kingdom come! Alleluia!

37. IMPARTIAL LOVE
Lord God, we thank and praise you that you love everyone equally. Help us to love with your impartiality, rather than with our partial loves; to love with your broadcast extravagence, rather than our small, restricted loves; and especially help us to try to love those persons we find hard and unsympathetic, for we are each and everyone a child of yours, and you love all your children. Praise be to you, O God.

38. FATHER
Father, your will be done; we trust you, tender, loving Father.

39. LOVE IS OUR BUSINESS
Almighty God, please help us to love all people, whether they be close to us or strangers, whether they be well-disposed to us or ill; please help us to love all activities, whether they be for maintaining the body or the soul, whether they be dear to our hearts, or necessary chores; and please help us to love all aspects of your creation, whether it be the bird that flies freely, or the bird we keep in a cage. Please help us to love all activities, all creatures, and, particularly, all people, that your will and your work may be done.

40. PRAYERS FOR WHEN WE ARE UNSURE
a. What shall I do now, Lord?
b. What shall I say, Lord?
c. Please help me, Father!
d. Please guide me, Father!
e. What is your will for me just now, Master?
f. What work would you have me do at this present time, Master?
g. Help me to love, O Lord!
h. Right now, O Lord? Right now, O Lord!

41. PRAYER FOR LOVE
Almighty God, help us to try to love our neighbour, help us to make the attempt, for we can only try, such are our limitations, such are our imperfections; and help us to accept that our attempts to love may be rejected. When these occur may we not try to overcome, to shout down as it were, the rejections of our attempts, but rather may we go on trying to love, humbly, caringly, patiently, that you, who are the God of love, may be made manifest!

42. ALL YOUR GIFTS
Almighty God, may we use all your gifts for your glory, for your service, not just our loving selves, our emotionally positive selves, but our intelligence, our will, our hands, our feet, our needs, our desires, all, Lord God, the whole of our being, given-up to your glory, to your work. Praise be to the God of all these things.

43. IN HIS PRESENCE
Almighty God, when we enter your presence may we stand straight before you, with the dignity and alertness appropriate to those who bear the title 'child of God', whose value is that ascribed by YOU, and whose hand is shaken by your own loving hand. Alleluia, we praise and thank you that we can enter your presence.

44. EASTER SATURDAY PRAYER

Almighty God, we praise and thank you for the life of Jesus, and in particular on this Easter Saturday we praise and thank you that he demonstrated by his appearances the continuation of life after death. Help us to enter into this new life as strongly and vibrantly as he did, and not sully ourselves by immoral and hurtful words and deeds, preferring rather, in preparation for it, to place our purity above all beliefs, aims and ambitions, however legitimate these seem to us. In a word, Father, help us to keep ourselves as morally wholesome as newly hatched chicks, that your name may be honoured.

45. UNMASKED!

Heavenly King, we recognise that we wear masks in daily life, and indeed the useful part that they can play, but we recognise also that when we come before you masks have no place, for you see us just as we are, as we really are.

We thank and praise you for the great privilege of coming before you, the ultimate reality, that reality which can provide for us the true centre to our lives, the true basis upon which to build them. We thank and praise you that we may come before you, the true reality, as we are, and open our hearts and minds to you, and for the fact that our weekly time of public worship gives us a tremendous opportunity to do so.

And lastly, Lord, we thank and praise you that, unmasked and open to the sweet emanations of your precious Spirit, we may become more attuned in our own spirits to yours, and may perhaps carry something of this growing likeness into our daily lives, that your work may be better done and your name more gloriously honoured.

46. REAL LOVE

Lord God, we have to love in ways which we understand, but are mindful that they may fall short. Guide us and illumine us to love in the ways in which you would have us love, and to seek the things which are truly good. Lord God, let our love be acceptable, and let the things

which are good in your eyes be the things we aspire to; so may we become God-centred. Alleluia!

47. GROWING-UP
Almighty God, we thank you for our individuation, and that through our development as autonomous individuals we may achieve the possibility of a proper relationship with you, and the maturing qualities of responsibility and independence. We praise you that our capacity for choice is demanded and respected. Thankyou for loving us tenderly as individuals throughout the hours and days of our lives! Alleluia!

48. STANDING STRAIGHT
Almighty God, we praise you for our individuation, for our blossoming as self-ordering beings, and we thank you that thereby we may achieve a genuine relationship with you, and responsibility for our conduct and decisions. We praise you that as unique persons we are loved uniquely, and thank you that your love is not occasional, but pursues us with great gentleness throughout our hours and days. Praise be to you!

49. A PRAYER FOR SUNDAY MORNING WORSHIP
Almighty God, we thank you for your warming sun and cooling wind, and your presence with us here this morning. We ask you that we may become instruments of your grace in all our relationships, in all our doings, during the week ahead.

50. IN YOUR GRACE
Almighty God, I pray that I may continue to live in your grace, in your love and mercy. I pray that I may try to achieve goals through rational thought and action, and that I may be the person that you would have me be in relation to all the people I meet on life's journey. I pray for these things as a being developing slowly, so slowly, in relation to you, the King of the Universe. Praise be to thee!

51. MY BIRTHRIGHT
Almighty God, I pray that I may accept my citizenship of your Kingdom as a little child, and that in doing so I may magnify your Name!

52. FOR THE HOLY SPIRIT
Almighty God, I humble myself before you a weak and silly person, and pray that you will send your Holy Spirit in power to help me to live as I ought, to do as I ought, in relation to you. Help me to be co-operative with you, to conduct myself fittingly and to work vigorously and effectively, that thus I may live in harmony with you, your creation and myself.

53. FOR WHEN WE ARE ENCOUNTERED BY GOD
Almighty God, I thank you for encounter with you; please help my response to be as rational, appropriate and sensible as possible.

54. LITTLE CHILDREN
Heavenly Father, Jesus said, "Suffer the little children to come to me." We are your children, and you love us as such, each and every one. You illumine us, guide us, protect us and convict us in our consciences. Let us come to you, trust you and share you today and everyday. We praise you for Jesus and his words!

55. TO BE GOOD (A)
Almighty God, please help me to be 'good' in relation to my girl(boy)-friend. Teach me what is good in such a relationship, whether it is to be kindly, considerate, sensitive, sensible, indeed, any appropriate good? As I say, please teach me.

56. TO BE GOOD (B)
Almighty God, please help me to be good in relation to my girl(boy)-

friend. Please teach me what are appropriate goods in a boy-girl relationship; show me your ways in this particular, important one. Thankyou, Lord.

57.   LET US TAKE OUR OPPORTUNITIES!
You address your children through your creation, Lord, through personal and community interests. When you so speak, help us to hear your voice. When opportunities come our way, help us to see them as such and to respond to them sensibly and positively, for in these is the stuff of your love for us, the expression of your purposes and wisdom.

58.   FORGIVE US, LORD
Almighty God, we pray that you will forgive us all the unkindness that we inflict upon one another, the physical and emotional hurts whereby we reduce the value of our neighbour. Let us be considerate of their feelings and avoid unkind laughter, indeed unkindness of any sort. We ask this for the sake of your kingdom, which we pray that you will help us to seek constantly.

59.   CITIZENS OF THE KINGDOM
Almighty God, we pray that, as citizens of your kingdom, you will help us to encourage all good things wheresoever we find them, and that also you will help us to discourage all evil things wheresoever we find them, impartially and indifferently in relation to all persons, whatever their relationship or their rank, as we go about our daily doings in this your wonderful kingdom, for, Lord, this world is your kingdom, and this life the life we have to live as its citizens.

60.   POINTING TO GOD
Lord God, please help me to point to you in all my doings today.

61.   GOD'S HATRED
Lord God, you hate me. Please help me to remember George Herbert's observation that, 'no perfect artist ever yet hated his own work.'

62.   ALL WORK AND NO PLAY
Almighty God, please bring me some love, some fun, some happiness, some enjoyable recreation and some fulfillment. Please Lord, at present life is all work and life support!

63.   THE MUSIC OF THE SPIRIT
O come, Most Holy Spirit, and fill our hearts and our minds, our bodies and our souls with your music, your wonderful music, the music of the Spirit! Alleluia!

64.   AS MYSELF
Almighty God, I thank you and praise you that you love me for myself, as an end in myself, rather than as an end to some further purpose; that you want me to do those things that I prefer to do, to do them well, and to have some fulfillment in doing them. Help me to love myself in that way, so that I may not frustrate your purposes of love, but co-operate fully in your guidance, your inspirations and your opportunities. Help me to value myself, even as you value me, for my worth is the worth which you set upon me, neither more nor less! Alleluia! Praise be to the one who loves his children!

65.   INFINITE LOVE
Almighty God, I thank you that love is not finite, that the more we give away the more we have, just like the magic purse in a fairy story, which however much is spent is always full. Lord God, I thank you that you are always ready to fill our hearts, minds and souls with the treasure of your spirit, with the invaluable pearl of your very self, so that, however much we manifest you, or try to do so, you are always at hand to render us

replete with new treasure, a fresh pearl of great price, to share and to enjoy with our fellow children. Alleluia, thank you, Father!

66. PROPER CONDUCT

Lord God, please help me to live my life day by day, hour by hour, minute by minute in proper ways, in ways appropriate for a child of yours, for a citizen of your kingdom! Let me speak and act thoughtfully, carefully, intelligently, sensibly, rationally and sensitively! In this way may your purposes of love be worked-out for myself and all your children, and for the whole of your creation, of your kingdom, that your name might be loved and respected, not ignored and defamed. Alleluia! Alleluia!

67. NEARER THAN HANDS

Almighty God, I thank you that your truth is close at hand, but that in your wisdom and your love for your children, you render it necessary for us to search it out; and I praise you for the paradox of this. Praise be to you!

68. PRAYER OF DEDICATION

Lord God, I dedicate myself to you. Please help me to remember that first and foremost all my doings must be pleasing and acceptable to you, must be right before you. Lord God, I dedicate myself to you. Please help me to live for you: you are wonderful! you are holy! you are beautiful! Alleluia!

69. A MEETING FOR WORSHIP THANKSGIVING

Almighty God, I thank and praise you for the wonderful outpouring of your light, your love, your life, your strength, your energy and your power, both directly through your Spirit with us in our Meeting House this morning, and indirectly through your creation, and in particular the rich beauties of this ebullient and blossoming Spring. Alleluia!

70.   THE TRUE REALITY, THE ETERNAL REALITY

Almighty God, I thank you that you are, that you are who you are and what you are, and that you are permanent, so that we can always turn and return to you, submit ourselves to you, knowing that in you we have the true reality. Praise be to you! Alleluia! Praise be to you!

71.   TRUE JUDGEMENT, TRUE LOVE!

Almighty God, I thank you that your judgement of your children, their inner thoughts and intentions and their outward behaviour, is true and always so; I thank you that your love for your children, with their inner hopes, aims, ambitions and desires and their outward activities, is true and always so. Thank you for providing your children with a true judgement, a true love, which may be entirely depended upon, in which we can repose our complete trust. Thank you for being the same today and at all times in the future.

72.   TO BE A BLESSING

Lord, let me be a blessing this day.

          Wilf Wilkinson, Rector of Clifton, Nottingham.

Blessing: a channel down which God's love flows.

73.   IF

Lord,
If I go to the right, you will be with me,
If I go to the left, you will be with me;
If I choose correctly, you will be with me,
I f I choose incorrectly, you will be with me;
If I am loved, you will be with me,
If I am hated, you will be with me;
If I am an object of kindliness, you will be with me,
If I am an object of spitefulness, you will be with me;
.... add further pairs as desired................
Lovely Lord

Help me to be truly grateful for this.
You are the ever-present one!
You will be with me always!
Alleluia! Alleluia!

74. TRUE TREASURE
Almighty God, help me to rest in you, to be content in you, to value fully the riches of your grace, knowing that there-in I have found the treasure hidden in a field, the pearl of great price. Help me to really believe what I ask, and to live what I believe; that yours is the glory, for ever and ever.

75. BLESSED ART THOU
Blessed art thou, o king of the universe, who cleanses us with laughter and redeems us with a smile.
                      RABBI LIONEL BLUE (Prayer for the Day, 19-9-83)

76. CLEANSE ME!
So much rebellion in me, so much hardness,
So much harshness, so much coarseness;
Cleanse me, please, Lord!
Bring into me the power of your spirit,
That being cleansed and filled by it,
I may be truly human,
I may be truly divine!

77. ALWAYS WITH GOD
Almighty God, I thank and praise you that I am always with you and that this helps to bring acceptance of my present situation and contentment in it. For whatever reasons, through whatever errors of judgement, and whatever lack of love in others and in myself I find myself in any particular place at any point in time, you are with me. I praise you and offer my love to you for this wonderful fact. Alleluia!

78.   EVERPRESENT!

Almighty God, we thank and praise you that we can come before you at any time, night or day, and in any place, at home, at work, or travelling, and for any reason, for help, for guidance, or just to be and share with you! We thank and praise you that you will not turn a deaf ear to your children, particularly if our need is genuine, or our cause is for the common good, and that you will respond with your self, your very self, your most holy spirit! We thank and praise you for coming to us, and in coming to us bringing the many and varied and good things which are yours, the good things that you will that your children should have, your light, by which you enlighten and inspire us, your life and your love! We thank and praise you that thus our needs are met and your kingdom is extended! Alleluia!

79.   DEATH OVERCOME?

Almighty God, it is taught that Jesus atoned for our sins, and overcame evil and death, but is this teaching correct? Does death need overcoming? Surely it is just a biological event, although possibly attended it is true by distressing circumstances, both in the manner in which death may be brought about, and in the effects death may have upon those close to the person who dies, but in itself, Father, is death an evil? Surely not. Sleep is one of your many precious gifts, a pleasure in itself and a boon in the beneficial effects it accords us, and sometimes I think of sleep as a rehearsal for our permanent sleep. Surely this too, if not a pleasure, is a good and accords your creation benefits, and also those who die. We thank and praise you for dying, for brother Death and his several merits, not least that he ushers us into a new life, hopefully one which is closer to you, our Heavenly Father.

80.   DEATH OVERCOME!

Almighty God, we thank and praise you that Jesus overcame evil and death on the cross, and in particular do we thank you that he demonstrated in his resurrection appearances that life after death is lived in newness of life and that the misdeeds of benighted men are not of permanent effect. Praise be!

81. HIS GOOD GIFTS

Almighty God, we thank you for your presence with us, and for the fact that we shall always have your presence with us; we thank you too for our past experience of the activities of your most holy spirit in our lives, for the light and love and life which you have brought to our hearts and minds, to our relationships, to our various interests and activities; and we thank you that this experience gives us hope for the future, knowing that as you have treated us in the past, always right, always to be trusted, so will you treat us at all times in the future. Almighty God, we thank you for these invaluable gifts: our trust in you, our hope in you, and the love we have in you.

82. THE BEST FORM OF PRAYER?

Almighty God, I feel at a distance from you. I have realised that when I speak or do that which is unacceptable to you, I take myself away from you, out of your house, as the prodigal son took himself off from his father and into a far country. Humbling myself before you, I come in penitence, wondering whether or not this is the best form of prayer. Am I not bringing myself into the ambit of your mercy, of your forgiveness and love - is it really true that you always forgive? Do you always run outside your gate to welcome the child who returns, weak and wilful though he has been? I thank and praise you for the gift of being sorry for our wrongdoings, and for the light by which you discover them to us. Surely coming humbly and in penitence before you is the best form of prayer! Are we not enabled thereby to come into your presence, to draw closer to you and to receive the regeneration which our brokenness makes possible? Alleluia, praise be to thee, O God, the God whose judgement is true!

83. TRUST HIM!

Almighty God, please could you help me in respect of any enterprise, of any job of work, of any dialogue, of any relationship, to seek and to find your will, to feel your wind blowing on my face, and to know and to rejoice that it is taking me in the direction and to the destination dictated by love. Alleluia!

84. ALL THINGS IN LOVE

Almighty God, whatever the enterprise I am pursuing, or the job of work to be done; or whatever the relationship, or dialogue, I am sharing; please could you help me to think in love, to carry my thinking into words and actions in love, and to bring both to fulfillment in love. Please could you help me, Father, to initiate and to continue and to complete all things in love, that your will may be done and your name honoured.

85. THE TRUE ROCK

Lord God, I thank you heartily that if I try to build the house of my life and soul upon the rock of your holy spirit, then I truly have all that matters. I may not have the job, the home, the family that I wish to have, or, indeed, might have had had I conducted myself more sensibly, but in having you as the foundation I have the proper, the best one. Praise be! Open my eyes to the certainty of your everlasting presence, the true rock, without which my house would crack and crumble into dereliction.

86. TO POINT TO YOU

Lord God, as the colt carried Jesus into Jerusalem, so may I carry you into the world, this day and for evermore.
(See Mk 11, vv8-10)

87. A PROBLEM? A SOLUTION?

Almighty God, we thank you for the ineffable sunshine of your holy spirit. When we play a game of chess we seek the continuation which will bring about the downfall of our opponent. Would you please grant us a continuation in this matter (state particular one) which is acceptable to you, which forwards your loving purposes, and would you please show us the continuation clearly, its strategy and its justification, that we might co-operate rationally and successfully. To this end help us to recognise your sunshine and to take it very seriously, that we might go forward confident in the love of all for their own sake, and imbued with your light and warmth. Help us to pray hard, think hard, to seek your guidance and to implement it, that your purposes and ours in yours, may find victorious accomplishment. Alleluia, Father!

88. AS A CHILD

Heavenly Father, a child can put themselves into another person's shoes so completely, be it soldier, nurse or mother. Help us to have a like imagination, so that we may increase our understanding of and sympathy for the position of others, and thereby promote peaceful relationships. Help us also to put ourselves into your shoes, Father, that we might better appreciate your situation and outlook. Alleluia!

89. SUNSHINE!

Almighty God, we praise and thank you that you are, and that you are who you are, and that we may come before you in our times of worship and open our hearts and minds to the sunshine of your Spirit, receiving your illumination and warmth thereby. Alleluia! praise be to you, O God.

90. THANKS BE TO THEE!

Almighty God, I thank you for your mercy, love and grace to me; and I thank you also for the greatness and wonder and beauty of your creation. Thank you, O God.

91. THE WORK OF LOVE

Holy Spirit, I am your servant and your child. Help me to embody you, and to do the work that you would have me do, your work of love.

92. A THANKS FOR INSPIRATION

Almighty God, I thank you for visiting your children with encouragement, illumination and guidance, through the power of your Spirit. I thank you that in this visiting you reveal your good self to your children, and enable them thereby to get to know you. And I thank you whole-heartedly that these visitations are those of a loving Spirit, that they do not undermine or replace in anyway the vigorous, rational conduct of the self, but rather support and inspire its activities. Alleluia to the God who loves his children!

93. WONDERFUL THANKS!

Almighty God, I thank you that I have not passed through your world without thanking you for some of its innumerable, beneficent aspects. Poor would I be indeed, if I did not thank you from time to time for these precious gifts. Father, I thank you most heartily for thanksgiving; life is indeed enriched by such small remembrances! Alleluia!

94. FRUITFUL LIVES!

Almighty God, we thank you that you see us as we are, our shortcomings, yes, but also the many potentialities we have for all sorts of attainments. Help us to recognise your words of love, Father, your words of illumination, encouragement and opportunity, and recognising them to respond to them in thoughtful, sensible and constructive ways, that they may be fruitful rather than blighted, and our lives be enriched rather than unfulfilled. So in all things may your work of love be our happiness. Alleluia!

95. WELCOME, MOST HOLY SPIRIT!

Almighty God, we open our hearts and minds to your spirit, placing before them a large card spelling out 'Welcome' in cheerful colours, for we know we may repose complete confidence in the goodness you bring, in the truth you manifest, and may go forward surely in their illumination. 'Welcome, most holy spirit!' We praise and thank you that you enable us to be your representatives, doing the work you would have done in fitting ways! Alleluia!

96. A PRAYER FOR GREATER FEELING AND SENSITIVITY

Almighty God, we ask that you will pour down upon us the blessings of your Light, your Life and your Love, and that by their power you will inspire and invigorate our hearts and minds to love and serve you and ourselves with greater feeling and sensitivity. Father, give us capacious hearts and minds, in which your Spirit may move powerfully and by which we may be the children you would have us be.

97. THANKS FOR THE HIDDEN SOURCE

Heavenly Father, we thank you for the all-seeing Love, the laser sharp Light and the fecund Life with which you have been graciously pleased to imbue our hearts, minds and bodies. We heartily thank you for this activity, praying that you will continue to imbue us so, and that we may go forward in the ways suggested thereby. Thank you, loving Father!

98. GOD KNOWS BEST

Heavenly Father, help us to realise that as children our experience and understanding are limited, while in contrast your perceptions are, to put it mildly, informed and comprehensive. When you reveal them to us may we open our hearts and minds to them, give them their true value and be guided by them. Help us to try not only to love you, but to be loved by you, that we may be the beneficiaries of the love you have for each one of us. Alleluia, Father!

99. PARTICULAR LOVE

Almighty God, we are sorry we have not realised that you love us and how much, doing so with a sensitive and particular love in respect of the various situations we meet day by day. Help us to recognise your love and to respond to it in sensible and practical ways, clear that we do so within the limits of your leadings. Praise be to the One whose love for his children is so great!

Sunflower

100. THE GREAT OAK

Father, we thank you that we are branches upon your great oak, and being so are suffused with the sap of the spirit, of the goodness, which wells-up within. Let us remember our divine attachment, that we are so suffused, and show forth the leaves and flowers of your divine life. Father, we thank you for the privilege, through co-operative behaviour, of having the opportunity to give substance to your great needs and purposes. Alleluia!

101. OBEDIENCE

Father, help us to direct our lives upon those principles of action which enable us to show forth the great love you have for all your children, and to utilise our gifts of intelligence and emotion for the expression of your holy spirit embodied in us. Help us to nourish our inner selves also by daily submission to you in worship, promoting thereby the flow of your good spirit! Alleluia!

102. GREAT JUDGEMENT!

Almighty God, we thank you for your judgement upon us, since your judgement is true. It opposes what we should not do and promotes what we should, both for our own sakes and that of others. Help us to accept your judgement and be guided in our conduct and activities by it.

103. THE BEST NOW

Almighty God, we thank and praise you for your totality, that you are in all space and through all time and being so are always and everywhere to be found; whatever our present situation, and for whatever reasons we are in it, we are equally with you. Heavenly Father, we praise and thank you for this. Help us to see that in our continuing relationship with you we have that which really matters, that which is best, at this moment, now. Alleluia!

104. BLESSINGS ABOUNDING!
Almighty God, pour down your blessings and help us to be ever striving consciously to be their instruments in relation to one another, and to be ever ready to take-up those specific calls to action which you lay upon us. Thus may your blessings be bountifully multiplied and your children's lives enriched immeasurably. Alleluia!

105. WE PRAISE YOU!
1. We praise you
That you are the one
Who has been from time beyond estimation
And still are!

First, second and fourth lines remain the same; the third line is replaced as follows:
2. Who has been with your creation at all times
3. Who has been discovered and known by men
4. Who has been turned to by men in every situation
5. Who has been depended upon and trusted by men
6. Who has been found entirely sound in judgement in all things
7. Who has been rested in at difficult times

Further lines may be added. Then to conclude:
We praise you
That you are the one
Who has been the source of hope in every vital matter,
And still are the same yesterday, today and forever.
Alleluia! Alleluia! Alleluia!

106. GET UP AND GO!
Almighty God, grant that we may have positive attitudes towards ourselves, attitudes of self-belief, confidence and drive, that we may pursue and make progress in our chosen concerns and interests. And may

we have positive attitudes towards you, that we may be co-operative in your designs of love for us, that your purposes, and ours in yours, may be fulfilled and not frustrated! Praise be!

107. ALWAYS CHILDREN

Father, I thank you that we are always children in our relationship with you, and that wonder, discovery and learning are always a natural part of it.

108. SOURCE OF LIFE!

Almighty God, we thank and praise you for the unviewable sun, for the nuclear furnace at its centre pouring forth the energies which make life and its development on our planet possible! Alleluia to the God whose great universe shows forth his greatness!

109. SMALL TASKS, GREAT TASKS!

Almighty God, enable me to take-up the great tasks which you make available as opportunities and challenges, to this end helping me to see that they are in fact many small tasks, albeit a long term, on-going series of them, within my competence, or which may be made so, through your guidance and my intelligent efforts. As each ear of wheat contributes to the expansive fullness of a cornfield, so may each small piece of work wrought well bring the great piece to fruitfulness, contribute to its beauty and wholesomeness. Living God, help me to do small tasks well, that added together they may become the great tasks. Alleluia!

110. ALWAYS PRESENT!

Praise be to you, O Heavenly King, that you are with your children and always ready to assist them. Praise be to you! Let your illimitable resources be our resources today, that in all endeavours and in all relationships we may apprehend your love, and, apprehending it, may seek truly to realise it. Praise be to the One who is always present! Alleluia!

111. LET LOVE RULE!

Heavenly Father, be present in our hearts today, that thereby they may be made worthy of your presence and the presence of your children, and enabled to enfold both in love.

112. TO INCARNATE AND EXPRESS THE SPIRIT

Today (1-8-83) I felt I should try to incarnate the holy spirit, that this was my purpose in life. I felt also that being imbued with the holy spirit I could to some extent express its character and purposes in my behaviour and actions. I was reminded of the list of 'goods' I had compiled, which I could pursue (although, like everything else, it lies forgotten). Anyway the following prayer is based on a real religious feeling and experience, even profound one, in that I felt I had (at last) really arrived at what is my purpose, my true purpose, in life.

Almighty God, I pray that I may incarnate your most holy spirit, and this being so, that I might be imbued with your character and qualities and express these and your purposes in my everyday behaviour and work, at all times and in all places and situations; thus might I be an honorable citizen in your kingdom!

113. BROTHER SUN

Almighty God, we thank you for the unviewable sun, which, with its vast, incandescent energies, makes possible life's continuity and development, its nuclear furnace pouring out the energies which cradle and nurture all that lives. We praise and thank you for your unviewable sun! Alleluia!

114. ALWAYS PRESENT!

Heavenly King, I thank and praise you that you are with your children, and, while their enemies would try to harm them, are always ready to help them. Be my resource today, in all situations and in all relationships, for your way, your guidance, is right and right to be implemented. Help me to do this, though far behind you I lag. Alleluia!

115. THE PRESENCE OF GOD

Almighty God, I thank you that all moments are of equal value and contain within them all the power, beauty, truth and love with which you are pleased to invest them, and which are coherent with your loving purposes. I thank you that we always have you with us, that we are always in your presence and the recipients of the wonderful gifts which it is your holy will to bestow upon your children. Thankyou! Alleluia!

116. POWER IN PRAISE!

Heavenly Father, I come before you to thank you that we can pray for the dark, distressing sides of our lives, and that we may not only seek your involvement in these aspects, your loving guidance, but may positively praise and thank you for the darkness, the evil condition, which hurts and harms us. How this can be I do not understand, and even more I do not understand how or why our praise and thanksgiving release the healing balm of your Spirit, the illumining, renewing, uplifting, enabling activity he occasions. Incredibly, when your child praises you for the most painful things, healing comes with power upon him. Such power in praise! Thank you, Father, thank you.

117. THE TWENTY BILLION LOVE

Heavenly Father, we thank and praise you for the fact that we may relate to you as a child does to its parent. Thank you, Father. We recognise the tremendous love which has made it possible for us to be here at all, for example, in the astounding bio-chemical engineering necessary for even the simplest life forms to have existence. Help us to love you just as you are. It is not easy, Father, even to think of loving you, such is the inveterate nature of our day to day concerns. Help us to love your children, our brothers and sisters. Grant also that we may accept that loving you and your children will necessarily entail, things being as they are, pain and suffering, even crucifixion. In accepting these, may we keep our love whole for you and for everyone who is a child of yours. Praise be to you, Father, who loves his children and rejoices in the love which they share with you and with one another. Alleluia!

118. CHOOSE THE RIGHT, NOTWITHSTANDING ANY OPPOSITION

In our distress, O Lord, grant us the discernment to see the good things of yourself, the things you have given us and the positive possibilities you have set before us. Grant us also the perception to see the evil things, the negative aspects of our lives, the things which nullify, frustrate, even destroy, our personhood. By the power of your Spirit illumine, guide and uphold our attempts to choose the helpful, the positive and the creative, and to eschew the hurtful and the destructive. Contribute your wholesome influence to our choosing, Father, in which we shall try to show strength of character and courage. In our distress, O Lord, grant that we may choose the good rather than the evil, the creative rather than the destructive, life rather than death, that we may live fully as a child of yours.

119. TWO TRIPLES

Lovely Lord, help us to see you more clearly, understand you more truly, abide by you more closely, this day and for evermore.
Heavenly Father:
we are your children,
teach us to worship you,
both in our public services,
and in our private devotions;
we are your children,
help us to love you,
for your self, and for the ways
you have provided for your children to journey;
we are your children,
lead us to recognise what you have done for us
in our incredible evolutionary development,

and in the manifold gifts this has made possible;
we are your children: alleluia! alleluia!

120.   FATHER, WE HAVE DONE WRONG

Heavenly Father, we thank you that having done that which is wrong in your eyes we may confess our wrong-doing. In our sin we have travelled from you, have entered a distant land, but in recognising our sin and in confessing it to you, we return to you and the other members of our family. Help us not only to say we are sorry, but to be sorry, to feel sorry; help us also not to think by saying sorry we bring the matter to an end, but rather let our penitence continue in our hearts and minds, recognising that if there is to a be a conclusion to the matter, it is within your sphere of responsibility, not ours, to provide it; and help us to remain open to you, open to the light you will provide in relation to our wrongdoing, and to implement your guidance and correctives. Heavenly Father, we thank and praise you for confession and penitence by which we may renew and improve our relationships with you and other members of your family. Alleluia!

121.   WE FOLLOW THE WAY RATIONALLY!

Lovely Lord, I thank you that our relationship with you is a co-operative one, and that you bestow the space in which we may marshall ourselves to do the things which you see fit for human beings to do. Help us to recognise these things and to try to do them in common-sense, rational ways, bringing as much effort and thought to your work, as many bring to activities which they conceive of as being their own.

Father, help us to conduct ourselves rationally, in the pursuit of your loving purposes and also in the solution of the problems which arise in that pursuit. It may be that some problems do not have solutions, but require that we approach them on a continuing basis in ways and with attitudes harmonious with your will. May we recognise and accept this state of affairs.

Let us respond to your guidance sensibly, recognising that you have spoken and seeking to understand what you have said and the reasoning behind it. If we do not understand your word, may we admit this and abstain from action and seek further guidance, in the meantime following our own judgement and reasoning.

Lovely Lord, I thank and praise you that we are called to conduct our lives rationally, and that to do so does not in any way shut you out, but includes your activities in relation to your children, so far as they may rationally be taken on board. Alleluia!

122. LISTENING TO GOD

HEAVENLY KING, we thank you and praise you that you speak to your children.

We thank and praise you that you take a personal interest in all the affairs and doings of your children and speak pertinently and helpfully in connection with them.

Help us to listen to you, and to recognise and incorporate your voice and love.

HEAVENLY KING, we thank and praise you that you speak to your children. Alleluia!

123. GOD SPEAKS

Lovely Lord, I thank and praise you for the many wonders in this wonderful world, and I thank and praise you especially at this time for one of the greatest, that you do indeed speak to your children.

Great is the impact of your Spirit upon our hearts and minds and bodies, creating there a marvellous array of messages, ideas and guidance!

Great is the ingenuity by which you speak through your creation and lead your children to hear, and see, what you know is pertinent for us to hear and see!

And great is the love by which you bring us by power and persuasion to be vehicles of this love, voices of this same love!

Alleluia! I thank and praise you, Lovely Lord, for the fact of your address to your children, wonder of wonders!

124. LOVE THE WAY FORWARD

Heavenly Father, we thank and praise you
that you are a god of love;
that you have a loving attitude
and conduct yourself in loving ways
towards your children;
that you lead, inspire and encourage us
to conduct ourselves in like manner
towards one another, showing us thereby
that in intelligent loving we have
a sure way forward in our relationships.
Heavenly Father, we thank you
for the love which finds its source
in your mercy: may it continue to foster
the unique hybrids which spring-up
between us, so that they may flourish
and flower, bringing happiness
and fulfillment to your children,
and honour to yourself.
Father, we thank and praise you that you are a God of love!

125. THE LORD IS JUDGE!

Lovely Lord, we thank and praise you that you are judge in all matters great and small, that while we have our views as to what constitutes good and bad, you too see things in a similar way from your own point of view. We thank and praise you that your judgements are always true, always correct, always good, always an expression of love, and being so may be viewed with pure pleasure and great joy. Help us to seek your view in all matters, and when you speak help us to receive your word with confidence and take steps to implement it sensibly. Lovely Lord, we thank and praise you that we may live our lives confident that your judgement will be righteous and wholly acceptable in our eyes. Alleluia!

126. GOD'S PURE LOVE

Dear Lord, we thank and praise you for your pure love, for the fact that your actions in relation to us have as their sole motivating force the good of your children; we thank and praise you for this, and for the fact that you consider not only the recipients of your loving activity on any particular occasion, but all your other children too.

Lovely Lord, we thank and praise you for your pure love.

Assist us in understanding that in following you we must try to love with a similar purity and impartiality, always acting for the good of all others and of ourselves, and always eschewing whatever is to a person's hurt, whether physically, mentally or spiritually.

Dear Lord, we thank and praise you for your pure love!

127. IN PRAISE OF THE FACT THAT THE POINT AND PURPOSE OF LIFE IS LOVE

Lovely Lord, I praise and thank you for the fact that the point and purpose of life is love;

that the manifestations of your most holy spirit in our lives are ones of love;

and that at all times we may seek to act in ways which serve your holy purposes of love.

Gracious Father, for the fact that the point and purpose of life is love,

I praise and thank you.

128. A PRAYER WRITTEN ON NEW YEAR'S EVE, 1987

Heavenly King, I thank and praise you for the year past, for all the good things which you wanted and made possible for your children, particularly those for whom I pray. It cannot have been easy for you to bring your precious gifts into our lives, such are our imperfections. Such love, but such imperfections! Help us in the coming year to love you for your own sake, and all your children for their own sakes and for yours. Heavenly King, help us to love in the coming year!

129. A PRAYER FOR CLEANSING

Lovely Lord, with the powerful powder of your Spirit, shosh me into the washing machine of your forgiveness, tumble and trumble me, spin and drin me, so that dropped dry, ironed and ired, new pin neat and clean, I may once more be worn to adorn your love.

130. PRAYER FOR GUY FAWKES' DAY

Heavenly Father, plant in us the desire to secrete the dynamite of love in the crypts below our national, local and personal governments, and having secreted it may we detonate it, bringing nearer government for reform and growth in our nation, in our communities and in ourselves.
B......R.......O.......O........M..........!.........!.........!

131. LOVING GOD FOR HIS OWN SAKE

Heavenly King, incredible light, multitudinous life and everlasting love:
help us to value you for your own sake, the Glory crowning a universe of glories;
help us to follow you for your own sake, conducting ourselves in ways which befit the dignity of a subject of such a King;
and help us to love you for your own sake, that we might love you even as we are loved by you.
Heavenly King, clothed in wonders, grant our petitions we beseech you!

132. PRAYER OF THANKSGIVING FOR OUR INDIVIDUALITIES

Lovely Lord, I thank and praise you for touching us with your most holy spirit, for spotlighting our inner selves, our own particular personalities; I thank and praise you for the appreciation this gives us of their uniqueness and worth to you and your world;
Lovely Lord, I thank and praise you for valuing your children for themselves, and the renewal of vigour and confidence to which this gives rise. ALLELUIA!

133. PERHAPS UNIQUELY

Almighty God, we thank and praise you for the inestimable gift of being able to worship you;

perhaps uniquely in a vast universe we, the created, can bow our heads before you, the Creator;

perhaps uniquely we can be the recipients of your spirit speech, each word personal, illumining and pertinent;

and perhaps uniquely we have the capacity to appreciate the love which informs each word, particularly with the passage of the years.

Almighty God, we thank and praise you for the inestimable privilege of being able to worship you; help us to take those opportunities we have of doing so and to place an appropriate value upon such a wonderful and benign gift. Alleluia!

134. LOVE, THE HEART

Almighty God, I thank and praise you that the essence of your nature is love, that unlove has no place in it.

I thank and praise you that all your dealings with your children are expressions of your nature, pure love, holy love, that unlove has no place in them.

And I thank and praise you that in our own conduct we are called on to clothe your nature with thoughts, words and deeds which make it a reality in the world, that unlove has no place in it.

May we incarnate your nature perfectly, even as you yourself are perfect. Alleluia!

135. ALL THINGS WORK TOGETHER

Almighty God, I praise and thank you for your attempts to love us, and through us those amongst whom we live. I am sorry that we have resisted your attempts, have failed to recognise them, and in general have failed to capitalise on them. May we learn from our past failures, and in the future try to respond sensibly and positively to your attempts to love us. Help us to be content with our present relationship with you, resolving always to be guided by you when you express your loving words in relation to us, and thanking and praising you that, if we love you, you can bring good from our ineptitude, that you can indeed make straight writing notwithstanding our crooked lines.

136. ENTER, O SPIRIT
Almighty God, may I be open to your Spirit, as an open door;
please enter in to do the work within me that you wish to do,
and remain, that today I may do the work that you wish me to do,
and be the person you wish me to be,
expressing myself suitably, pointing to you thereby,
which is my daily task, my vocation,
deputed by you, our Heavenly Father.

137. LOVE BINDS ALL
Heavenly Father, I thank and praise you that love is the central characteristic of your nature, and that all its characteristics are unified and bound by it.

138. MYRIAD MIRACLES!
Heavenly Father, I thank and praise you
for the myriad evolutionary miracles,
which have made my existence possible;
for the myriad developmental miracles,
which have given me form;
and for the myriad sustaining miracles,
which uphold and enrich my being
in every way. Alleluia, Father!

139. HELP US TO VALUE
Almighty God, help us to value the good things in life, the small things as well as the large, the things that we can experience, and the things that we can do;

help us to value the good things in life, so that we may make the effort to experience them, and to bring them into being;
and help us to value the good things in life, so that we see that it is worth making the small efforts necessary to bring the small, good things into being, and that the large good things are generally the result of many increments of these same small, good things.

140.   PRAYER FOR THE PROPER USE OF SHORT PERIODS
Heavenly Father, we thank and praise you for the good things of life, and that we have it within our scope to bring them about by practical, rational action.
Help us not to pass-up short periods of action through thinking that since they are short they are not worth initiating.
Small steps may be taken in them, fresh things learned and new discoveries made. We shall after all only do something else, and a particular opportunity will have been lost, and perhaps the time available will have been wasted too; and time, some think, is your most precious gift!
Thank you, Heavenly Father, for the good things you have made it possible for us to experience, and the manageable efforts in short periods of time we may initiate in pursuit of them.
Indeed, the small achievements in such shorter periods may take their place among the good things which it is your gracious will we should enjoy! Alleluia, Heavenly Father!

141.   THE UNACCEPTABILITY OF SMALL EVILS
Oddly, Lord, you are against small incidents of wrongdoing, as well as their larger counterparts. I suppose this is not surprising, since wrong is wrong and cannot be acceptable to one whose judgement is finer than an eye surgeon's laser. I suppose, when you think about it, wrong-doing is harm-doing, and harm-doing is what evil is about, and evil of whatever dimension must be unacceptable to one who is perfect, to one who is good. I suppose that while the odd cigarette may not give you lung cancer, it may have slightly harmful effects, and could lead onto greater

wrong-doing, such as heavier smoking, or encouraging some-one else to smoke or to continue smoking. I suppose, then, it is not surprising you are against even small increments of wrong-doing, such as the occasional cigarette, and that we may reasonably extrapolate that you are against harm-doing, small-scale as well as large, of whatever kind.
Not oddly, Lord...!
Have mercy upon us, forgive us all our wrong-doings, and help us not to tolerate in ourselves even evils which appear to be small-scale in their effects, but to set our eyes firmly on the target of being against evil in all its forms, the smaller ones as well as the larger. Lord, have mercy upon us.

142.   PRAYER TO BE FIRM (A)
Almighty God, help us to stand firm for what is right, for what is beneficial to people, and equally to be firm in our opposition to what is wrong, to what is harmful to people. We are all of equal value in your eyes, Father, and all should be treated correctly, dealt with rightly and constructively. May whatever we do in relation to anyone benefit them. With this fundamental principle clear in our eyes let us act positively in promoting what is right and in opposing what is wrong, not allowing social pressures of any kind to weaken our witness, or to deter us from it. Father, we beseech you, uphold and support us that your name might be freely honoured.

143.   PRAYER TO BE FIRM (B)
Almighty God, help us to be firm and confident in our loving of people. Help us always to think in terms of the individual, of what is best for them, whatever the aspect of their lives which concerns us at the present. If we have to oppose a person in some matter let us do so in such a way that we are clear that we do so for that particular individual's benefit, rather than for some less personal ideal. Let us not be put-off by people who read our attempts to be positive and loving in less than kindly ways, but go forward along the road of life firm and confident in our loving of all your children. Alleluia!

144. SELF-DETERMINATION WITH SENSITIVITY TO THE HOLY SPIRIT
Heavenly Father, we thank you for the gift of freedom and for the possibilities it entails of self-direction and personal decision-taking.
Help us to utilise these possibilities fully and responsibly; but let us not use them in ways which exclude you, in ways which, because the hatches of our hearts and minds are battened down, keep-out the invasive power of your spirit. It is right to exclude the endangering waters of the seas, but we should not resist the ministrations of your spirit, which is the spirit of love. Help us to welcome them, and not forget their objective, which is the fulfillment of our legitimate needs and desires, hopes and aspirations, and your purposes for all your children. Alleluia!

145. A PRAYER TO HEAR GOD
Almighty God, I thank you that we enjoy the polarity of a relationship, that you act in the ways peculiar to yourself, and that I have the privilege of being an autonomous self. Help me to exercise my autonomy in an intelligent, sensitive and light-reined way, so that when you speak, whether it be a quiet whisper, or a powerful enthusing of the spirit, I am able to take on board what you say, rather than reject or ignore it, be frightened or caused to feel resentment by it. Let me thereby be an instrument of your spirit, strongly acting, but rightly acting in your eyes. Alleluia!

146. RESPONSIBLE AUTONOMY
Lovely Lord, I thank and praise you for the relationship we enjoy, and for our mutual autonomy. Help me to exercise my own in a responsible way, and not to set aside your words, whether whispers or powerful enthusings of the spirit, through fear or impetuosity.

147. LOVING SERVICE
Almighty God, help me to work for the benefit of your children,

especially spiritually. Help me to make positive observations about yourself, and our relationships with you, your children and your world. May we be a closer knit, more happy family, and to this end may we be more knowledgeable about and more loving towards one another. Alleluia!

148.   DIVINE LIGHT
Almighty God,
may we look upon your light with one another,
may we share your light with one another,
and may we live in your light with one another.

149.   YOUR LIGHT
Almighty God, may we look upon your light with one another;
may we live in your light with one another;
and may we share your light with one another;
so that our beings may be filled with light,
so that our lives may be expressions of light,
and so that our relationships may grow in light
rather than darkness.
Glory be to you, who is light and the source of light;
Glory be to you, whose light redeems us,
whose light guides us, whose light nurtures us,
and in whose light we have our dwelling for ever.
Almighty God, may we look upon your light!
Alleluia! Alleluia!

150.   PRODIGIOUS!
Almighty God, we thank and praise you for your bountiful love:
for a love which has involved preparations on a prodigious scale in time and complexity;
for a love which, notwithstanding the prodigious numbers of people who share our planet, is particular to each individual, his immediate

intentions and circumstances;
and for a love which is integral to our environment, and will continue to be with us as we tackle new ventures on our prodigious journey.
For this bountiful love, Almighty God, we thank and praise you!

151.   YOUR WILL BE DONE
Almighty God, we pray for a right understanding of what characterises your will for your children, and the different ways in which it may find expression; we pray also for a right understanding of how we may seek to know your will for your children, in general and in particular situations, and of how we should try to put it into practice.
We recognise that there are many temptations in respect to trying to be a faithful child of yours, that self-delusion is only too easy in this matter. Bring us through these temptations to a right understanding of your will, which is your love for everyone, and to the knowledge which enables us to implement it in sensible and sensitive ways,
that your will may be truly done this day and forever.

152.   YOU REMAIN WITH ME
Lovely Lord, I thank and praise you that you remain with me.
Whatever decision I take, whether right or misguided, opportunity-taking or opportunity-missing, you remain with me;
whatever situation I am in, whether most appropriate to your purposes of love, or otherwise, you remain with me;
you remain with me, seeking to uphold your love and purposes for me through guidance and opportunity, enlightenment and inspiration.
Lovely Lord, I thank and praise you that you remain with me.

153.   TO HANDLE OUR IDEAS
Heavenly Father, it is strange the way ideas pop into our minds, good, helpful ideas and also, unfortunately, hurtful ones too. It would be easy to believe that the good ones are triggered into the mind by the Spirit, and perhaps they are. There is no way of really knowing. While recognising

that we may not know the sources of our ideas, we do know what our duties are in respect to them, for example, that rational conduct is to be preferred to irrational conduct.

Heavenly Father, help us to keep our ideas subservient to the very best in us, the highest standards of internal organisation and moral rectitude, that at all times we may behave, within and without, according to the ways which you have planned and prepared for your children. Where our knowledge is deficient in this regard, could you please teach us more which is currently pertinent about them. We ask this that we do not become victims of self-delusion, for this way lies the disruption of your Kingdom, the jeopardising of your fullness of life, and the replacement of your joy with anxiety and fear. May your will be done

154. HEALTHY LIVING

Almighty God, we praise and thank you for the good ideas we have, for those which are pertinent and helpful to legitimate aspirations and goals; and we are sorry for the bad ideas we have, which, if implemented, would be hurtful to others and ourselves. We are not sure on what basis these ideas emerge in our minds; perhaps there is a subtle interplay between our inner beings and your most holy spirit. At all events help us not to waste our ideas, but rather let us utilise them as a part of the ongoing process of healthy, vigorous and rational living, in which our own needs and aims take an equal place besides those of others. Help us to be in charge of our ideas, rather than let them take charge of us, even for the apparently good cause of doing your will. We are sorry that we have allowed ideas to lead to the mismanagement of our lives, which in turn has led to anxiety and neurosis. Almighty God, we praise and thank you for pertinent and helpful ideas, for thereby your love is expressed, and in the implementation of which our lives are enrichened and fulfilled.

155. AGAINST SELF-DELUSION

Heavenly Father, we thank and praise you that you speak directly to your children in personal and pertinent ways. Your words cannot be imagined or forecast, yet we may try to kid ourselves that you have spoken in a particular regard, when you have not. Help us not to do this. Help us rather to understand, and to think hard and pray earnestly that we may understand, what it is that you have said, what is really on your mind to communicate to us. If we feel we have some understanding, may we implement our considered response in sensitive and sensible ways, that your love for your children may come to a proper fruition! Alleluia!

156. TO CONTINUE ATTEMPTING TO LOVE

Almighty God, please help me to accept the fact that my good will towards others will not necessarily be welcomed or responded to. You have attempted to love me over the years and I have rejected your love more often than not, yet you have not given-up speaking and acting for my good. Help me to continue attempting to love. Also, help me not to resent the fact that life seems to be little else than work, but rather see that work is the means by which love is shaped, implemented and expressed, and that I am not so much an economic or work unit as a love unit! ONE LOVE UNIT! Alleluia!

157. INCARNATION

O lovely Lord, that we may incarnate you in our persons,
    INVADE US;
that we may incarnate you in our institutions,
    HELP US;
and incarnating you may we receive and express
    YOUR POWER,
    YOUR LOVE,
    YOUR FRIENDSHIP
in and through our persons and our institutions;
to the praise of your ineffable name!

158. WORKING FOR GOD

Lovely Lord, we look upon your great goodness and praise you;
we see your world as an instrument of your love for us and praise you.

Grant that we may recognise your will and work for us,
and recognising it, respond to it,
and perform it with alacrity and enthusiasm;
so may our lives join in with our tongues in praising you.
Alleluia! Alleluia! Praise be!

159.   OUR DAILY WORK
Gracious Lord, look favourably upon your child and his daily work; show him the right way forward in all situations, that he may be well and successfully employed in serving you and your children. May his work be suitable, as he earns his daily keep and works for your kingdom, and motivated by love, your love for everyone; and so may your name at all times be revered and honoured!

160.   OUR DIFFERENCES
Lovely Lord, help us to see all people as your children, even though we may not agree with their opinions, beliefs and general outlook in important matters; help us to accept and suffer such differences, and to give priority to having a loving attitude and maintaining constructive thought and action; that your will may be done and your name of Eternal Love be honoured! Alleluia!

161.   SERVING GOD
Lovely Lord, Heavenly Father, I thank and praise you for the perception that a God of love is served by acts of love. Help me to put the winning ways of love first, and not to allow those opposed to them to be given credence in my mind and heart. The temptations and demands which arise from within and without, from people and from institutional situations, can be overwhelming. Notwithstanding these, help me to give priority to love, to the love which lovingly transmutes itself into acts of love, and thereby give priority to you, your creatures and your creation! Alleluia!

162. GOD CAN ONLY BLESS

Lovely Lord, I thank and praise you that you bless your children, and indeed can only bless your children; that even your judgement of and opposition to them are expressions of your love, for you seek their good and can only be angered or disappointed by those things which do not contribute to this in some particular way. Help us to give-up all fears, of whatever kind, and to live positively, without worry or anxiety, knowing that we live in your blessing and can only live in your blessing, and rejoicing in this. Help us to be towards others and ourselves as you are towards us, pleased to be able to bless, and pleased to be instrumental in enabling some blessing you are seeking to bestow! Alleluia!

163. GOD CAN ONLY LOVE

Lovely Lord, we thank and praise you that you always act out of love for each of us, seeking our good in terms of our present situations and present level of knowledge and understanding. Praise be!

164. PRAYER FOR THE PREFERENCE FOR GOD

Heavenly Father, we thank you that, in the pursuit of your love for your children, you uphold their reasonable and proper aspirations, needs and concerns. Thank you for your love's implementation in your gifts of time, opportunity and means, which make possible the fulfillment of our aspirations and the meeting of our concerns and needs. Thank you also for your guidance and support. Help us not to allow our fears, and the real or imagined unlove inspiring some of these, to prevent our co-operation with you. When making our choices may we give preference to your loving goodness, your goodly loving, rather than to suspicion and hostility, and may we be prepared to suffer and accept the hurts which these inflict upon us. Let your will be done! Alleluia!

165. PRAYER TO KNOW THE WAY FORWARD

Almighty God, pour down upon us your light and inspiration, that we may know the way forward for our loving, the words that we must think and write and say, the things we must do and complete. Have mercy upon us, and extend to us the helping hand of your love and tender understanding. Thus may we progress satisfactorily in the work you have given us for the benefit of all your children: gracious Lord!

166. A PRAYER IN ANTICIPATION
Heavenly Father, I thank you for the wonderful gifts which you have granted to us week by week in our Meetings for Worship and Sunday School classes, gifts of inspiration and insight, of understanding and comfort; and I thank you for the wonderful gifts which you will be making possible for us today: in anticipation, thank you, Father, THANK YOU!

167. A PRAYER IN ANTICIPATION
Heavenly Father, I thank you for the wonderful gifts which you have previously granted to us day by day, gifts of inspiration and insight, understanding and comfort; and I thank you for the wonderful gifts which you will grant us today: in anticipation, THANK YOU, FATHER, THANK YOU!

168. FOR SHARING GOD'S LIGHT AND LOVE
Lovely Lord, we thank and praise you for the seed of your light and love in our hearts and bodies, minds and souls, and for the crops of increased knowledge and understanding which are raised from it. Help us to harvest these, to winnow and to mill them, and from the flour bake first class spiritual bread to distribute to all who wish to partake of it. Wonderful seed! Praise be!

169. A THANKSGIVING PRAYER FOR MY NEW AMSTRAD COMPUTER
Lovely Lord, I thank you for the Amstrad computer which you have

made it possible for me to possess. It is absolutely super! The Windows operating system which came with it is absolutely fantastic! The things which you can do with Windows are absolutely amazing! Dear Lord, my prayer may seem over the top, but I am as pleased as punch with my new purchase. Help me, please, to use my computer to service those activities which come within my remit, the honouring of your name and the doing of your will. For yours is the kingdom, the power, and the glory.

As it turned-out my prayer was in no way over the top. It was seven-and-a-half years before my monitor went, seven-and-a-half years which as far as the hardware went were absolutely trouble free. Oh, I forgot, I had to replace the mouse a year or two earlier. Great! More to the point it has been a valuable tool in helping me to do the things which I do for my work and recreation, writing, drawing and painting and singing!

170. O LOVELY LORD, COME QUICKLY!

'O Christ! come quickly.' This prayer was uttered by a nun when 'The Deutschland' was wrecked on a sandbar in the North Sea. The sentiment could be the basis for a more extended prayer. Here is one such, based on experiences in a Meeting for Worship at Leicester.

O Lovely Lord, come quickly! Come quickly and make your gentle presence known to us, that we may be upheld and our separateness dispelled. Gather us under the wing of your holy spirit, as a hen gathers her chicks, that we may find thereunder kindliness, strengthening and a peaceable unity. O Lovely Lord, come quickly!

171. CITIZENS OF THE KINGDOM OF GOD!

Lovely Lord, help us to have a care for one another's spiritual needs with as much readiness of thought and action as we have for one another's physical needs. To that end help us to see them as much a part of the everyday fabric of life as the readily accepted things, such as eating and drinking, and to speak about them with equal ease and pertinence. Lovely Lord, help us to have a care!

172. THE GARMENT OF LOVE

Lovely Lord, I thank you for clothing me in the Spirit's garments and in particular the garment of love. Its cloth is pure, pure as you yourself are pure! Its cut is the style sported by those in the swing of the Spirit! It dictates the garments worn with it and any accessories! Its line is soft, yet sassy, a pleasure to the eye! Lovely Lord, I praise you that you are our fashion, and that we may wear with pride the garment of love!

173. COLOSSAL LOVE

The following is a prayer of praise and thanksgiving based on the thought that love may be defined as the expenditure of time and energy in relation to a person or activity, beneficially rather than otherwise, of course. It was meditated in a Meeting for Worship at Winchmore Hill Meeting House, initially in relation to evolution, and subsequently and appropriately in relation to a holiday at Bembridge, on the Isle of Wight. In the latter connection I thought particularly of the brilliant sunshine and fresh air.

HEAVENLY FATHER, I thank and praise you for the massive expenditure of your time and energy upon your world; I thank and praise you for your great love of it.

174. LOVELIEST GIFT: PRAYER

After saying a Barbara Cartland prayer* with regard to the prayer I was hoping to write for this assignment, I decided it was time for a cup of tea. Kaleidoscope was on Radio 4, and a festival of traditional music from around the world was being reviewed. Singers from the States were harmonising, followed by Buddhist monks playing the music which had gone underground after the Maoist revolution. I thought that if we can accept the strangeness of these forms of expression, and of the religious expression in particular, we can accept the place of prayer. There is no

---

*I heard Barbara Cartland remark on the radio that before she began a new novel she said a prayer asking for an idea for the plot of it. She added that this was a prayer which was always answered.

need to fight shy of it at all! After all, a popular song invites us to sing our own song, and why should we not, there is none better!

Lovely Lord, I thank you for the wonderful means of expression we call prayer, for in it we can talk to one another, sharing with one another the matters on our minds, the matters currently of concern to us. Especially do I thank you for speaking to me, for by what you say you open my eyes, enabling me to see those things to which previously I had been blind!

> Amazing grace - how sweet the sound -
> That saved a wretch like me!
> I once was lost, but now am found,
> Was blind, but now I see.

175.   PURE LOVE!

Lovely Lord, I thank you for the concept of pure love, a love which suggests we hold others in high esteem, have a twinkling sense of humour, and are patient, content and good-natured. May this sentiment inform all the areas of our lives, our attitude towards ourselves, towards others, particularly those in whom we have a romantic interest, and our work. May all be the recipients of our tender, loving care, of completely unadulterated love. Pure love! Alleluia!

Some time ago Radio 4 did a series on the elderly and love, one programme of which was made up of reminiscences about departed partners. One lady, who was apparently very elderly, spoke with a deep, strong voice. She described her husband in the most affectionate terms. She used a particular phrase to indicate the nature of his conduct in relation to her, a phrase which must rank as one of the highest compliments which can be paid, and which punctuated what she said like a refrain. I cannot remember the reminiscences, but the phrase remains with me as an unforgettable experience, and hence the prayer above. It was 'pure love'.

176.   CAUSE AND EFFECT

Almighty God, open our eyes to see our situations in life as they actually are, and in particular their unsatisfactory aspects. We accept them, temporize about them and do not give them the serious attention they merit, but all conditions have consequences. As you see, eventually the hurtful ones take their toll and we are devastated and made disconsolate by them. Open our eyes to see and to face the unsatisfactory aspects of our lives, and help us to take the necessary rational, positive action to improve them. We cannot make our lives perfect, but we can try to make them better and try to lessen our pain. Please help us in this intention.

177.   SUFFERING

Almighty God, we believe that suffering is the coping strategy which you would have your children adopt in the face of evil. We would not wish to dwell on suffering, since it is not our aim to increase it, but we wish to confirm that we understand the place it has in the divine economy. We can see that in suffering evil we are not adding to it by retaliating with evil. We can see also that we have our minds concentrated solely on the good things we have in our window, and that it is these that we have on offer to a person and only these. Another may bring evil into our lives, but we must await their custom for the good things that we have for them to purchase from us. Lovely Lord, keep our minds firmly on the good things which we can supply and help us to value them highly, sufficiently highly to keep any evil things from intermingling with them. Let our stock be only of the best! Alleluia!

178.   SPIRITUAL PAIN

Lord, as you know, recently for no apparent reason I had an experience of acute pain in my emotional-spiritual body, and this has led me to consider this matter. In the face of the ills and evils of life physical pain has a positive role to play, in that, for example, it encourages us to take remedial action when the body is sick in some way. We do not like it, but we recognise that it is helpful. If we have a toothache, we get along to the dentist's! Am I correct in thinking that our spiritual pain also has positive functions, that at the very least it is necessary if we are to have consciousness at all. I would think that pain in our spiritual bodies is ordinarily an indicator that something is wrong, and that we ought to take steps to address the ill or evil which lies behind it. Help us, Lord, to face our spiritual pain and to take sensible steps to redress the sickness which causes it! Open our eyes, and reveal your healing touch! Alleluia!

179.   FOR MYSELF
Holy God, although you have made us for one another may I play my part in bringing into my life the good things rather than the bad, love, kindliness, consideration and truthfulness. May I see myself as an end in myself, of infinite value and your child. May I have pure love, Holy God, towards you, your world, your children and myself, and may that pure love point to your own strong and wondrous love!

180.   TO SEE GOD AS AN END ALWAYS!
LORD, help me to value you for your own sake, and to this end to be of an independent spirit in seeking to attain the various goals I have. May I look to my own efforts to deliver whatever my heart and mind are set on, rather than looking to you to do the job for me, even subconsciously – particularly subconsciously! Help me also to realise that "some will, some won't", that some efforts will be rewarded with success and some will not. Where they are not, let this be an indication to me to try to improve my strategies and skills and to be more determined in seeking the particular goal concerned. As I say, Lord, I ask these things in order that the temptation to see you as a means to an end might be reduced. I recognise, and praise and thank you for it, that you do seek to assist your children in their proper aims and make significant contributions to their efforts, for example, in guidance and opportunities. While making suitable use of them when they do occur, I ask that I may not look for these, but rather keep my love for you pure, valuing you in and for yourself at all times. Alleluia!

181.   HE WHO MANIFESTS HIMSELF!
O God, we thank and praise you that you manifest yourself without and within in order to achieve your loving purposes, but in doing so additionally reveal yourself thereby! Such manifestations help us to know that you exist and your eternal character! Alleluia! Alleluia!

182.   AT A FRESH START
Almighty God, recently I have had an important insight, and feel that I should have a period in which to re-assess myself and way of life, and grow and catch up in the light of my new understanding. While at this self-prescribed oasis would you please let me know how you would like me to conduct myself in future and what activities you think I should undertake. I realise that I cannot have a completely new start, since I have learnt a few things on the way, but if you wish to make any contributions to my reflections and considerations I should welcome them. In anticipation, thank you, Lord.

183.   A PROBLEM FOR GOD
Almighty God, I have a problem for you. You are said to be a god of love, a view with which I agree, since I think the essence of your being is love. I have enjoyed a long term relationship with you, during which I have worshipped you to a reasonable degree and worked for you, although not very successfully. During this long term relationship I have learned that I should seek to love you, rather than make demands upon you, and, in fact, I think that it is true to say I have not been particularly demanding upon you. Also, Jesus suggests that it is in order to make requests of our Heavenly Father Such requests that I have made have primarily concerned the possibility of having a girl-friend, with a view, eventually, to marriage, which brings me to the point of my prayer. Notwithstanding that you are love-god, and notwithstanding I have been relating to you day-by-day for many years, my life is, to all intents and purposes, devoid of love, love is virtually absent from it. This is not to suggest that the people I know are not ordinarily pleasant and considerate. They are. What I am talking about is the absence of a close, personal

relationship. How does this come about? Why are you so completely deaf to my prayers? If you are not completely deaf, why have you not helped me to deal with the psychological hindrances which have prevented me from forming a close relationship? The last time anyone had a care for me was fifty years ago, when I lived with my grandmother. As I remember it she liked me and cared for me. Since then more or less total barrenness has been my lot. You are a god of love and yet it appears to be in order for your children to live lives which are totally devoid of love. How can this be? Do we not matter to you? If we mattered to you, you would help your children to have the good things of yourself in their lives(★), as Jesus suggests, and surely a close, warm, loving relationship is one such, a relationship in which we can value a person and be valued in turn. As I say, it is a long time since I enjoyed such a relationship. How can this be? Do you not care, do you not love your children? How comes it that your conduct in relation to them is ineffective, so totally ineffective?

184. A BURNING QUESTION
Lord, I have a question for you. I have been your love-child during my life, and yet, notwithstanding this, it is and has been since childhood more or less devoid of human love. How comes this, Lord? If there is an answer to my question, please let me know what it is and help me to do something about it quickly!

You may not feel this particular burning question is appropriate for yourself. Perhaps you have one of your own!

185. DRESS FOR THE LORD
Lord, help me to put on
the undergarments of decency,
the shirt of good sense,
the necktie of friendliness,
the suit of humbleness and truthfulness,
the shoes of constancy,

(★) I typed 'loves' at first, but this was a typo. Still, food for thought!

the raincoat of kindliness,
and last but not least
the hat of courtesy,
that I may live in love
with all your children,
older and younger alike.

186.   ORDINARILY!
Lord, let me ordinarily be ordinarily constructive.

187.   LOVES!
Dear Lord, please help me today to see you, your children and your world as LOVES!

188.   PRAYER OF DEDICATION
Heavenly Father, by the power of your most Holy Spirit,
help me to bring love into being,
to bring truth into being and to bring beauty into being,
through appropriate attitudes,
through appropriate words and works and withholdings,
bringing thereby goodness into being, good into being, you into being!
pointing thereby to you,
whose essence is love and truth and beauty,
who is the essence of love and truth and beauty,
good in yourself, the good that is in all people and all things,
most Holy Spirit, most Holy Spirit incarnated,
Heavenly Father! Alleluia! Alleluia!

189.   FILL ME!
God of love! God of judgement!
fill me with your loving kindness!
fill me with your moral sensitivity!

and help me to bring them to bear in everything,
that in everything your holiness may be upheld!
Praise and thanks be to you,
God of love! God of judgement!

190.   A PRAYER TO EMPOWER THE SPIRIT!
ALMIGHTY
GOD,
THE
WORLD
IS
YOUR
KINGDOM!
HELP US TO RECOGNISE
THAT WE ARE ITS CITIZENS.
SO MAY YOUR VISION BE GIVEN!
SO
MAY
YOUR
SPIRIT
BE
EMPOWERED!
SO
SHALL
YOUR
KINGDOM
COME!
ALLELUIA!

191.   NEW PAINT FOR OLD
We get flaky, Lord, like old paint! We have sustained the splitting frosts and the cutting rains, and now, no doubt lacking sufficient durable ingredients, we have paled and dulled, have peeled and curled, and are

allowing the spores of decay to take hold within.

Burn-off the old paint, Lord, replace the decayed timber! Make us paints that will remain shiny, bright and firmly in place, to do the things we are meant to do for your home, freshly, positively, substantially, commitedly and well! Alleluia! Praise be!

192. A NEW PRAYER FOLDER - A NEW START

Lord, since I am starting a new prayer folder, I am taking the opportunity to reconsider my daily Quiet Time. I am particularly interested in the basic assumptions and attitudes underlying my approach to you in prayer. I feel I should be completely open in relation to you, and in order to implement this do not wish to place any restrictions on the time allowed for a given form of prayer and its supporting thought. At least in this approach you have the maximum opportunity to speak to me on any given matter, and for me to reach a clearly articulated expression of it in prayer and writing. Still, I can see that it is in order to leave a particular matter and return to it in the next turn of the cycle. Yes!

193. A CHRISTMAS PRAYER

Lord, you brought Jesus into the world as it was then: help us to bring your good things to birth in the world as it is and we are now.

194. 'THINK AND ACT POSITIVELY! LIVE THE GOOD LIFE!

Lord, help me to look for and to find the good things which life has to offer, to this end determining what are the good things that I should like to see in my life, and then making all such decisions and efforts necessary to seeing them actually realised in it. Help me to stay firm in my apprehensions and objectives, and also to accept that I shall feel low at times, that there will be times when I feel hopeless and despondent. In your mercy, Lord, help me to have a positive outlook, and to express it in positive thought and action. Achieved good things will add-up to a good life. As I heard a sixth former say on the radio about some poems she had heard, you have got to work to make your life the best it can be before you die. Truly good things will make my life not only a good one, but the best it can be! Alleluia, Lord!

195. MY GARDEN

Lord, you have given me a garden to tend, a garden where-in I can grow crops and flowers to feed and delight the inner man. As well as being a gardener I am also a chef, for from the kitchen I serve my writings and pictures as a tasty book or magazine, or display sometimes as a decoration. Lord, I thank you for my work. Help me to be pleased to do it, and to attend to it sensibly, and not to forget its aim: to feed and delight us all! Alleluia!

196. TO FACE BAD THINGS HONOURABLY

Almighty God, please help me to face the bad things which can happen to us, such as disease and its treatment, with courage and practical good sense, that I may cope with them and live through them as well as I am able. To you, O God, I give praise and thanks for a helping hand, human or divine! Thankyou!

197. St. MATTHEW 5 vv43,44

Lord, help me to bring a positive, constructive, kindly attitude and approach to people and yourself, whether we are sharing good things or evil, yes, even when we are sharing evil things. Please, Lord.

198. PEOPLE MATTER, LORD!

People matter, Lord, as you made clear in relation to my short-comings when looking after members of my family. Help me, therefore, to be a means of grace rather than a means of evil, such as, kindly rather than hard, and truthful rather than silent in a way which spells uncaring. Help me also to live consistently in the light of this notion: people matter! Lord, praise be!

Clock House at Thorpe Satchville

199.   PEOPLE MATTER
People matter.
Help us, O Lord, to care for and behave towards people properly, decently and responsibly, all people, whatever they may have said or done, or not, in relation to us.
'People matter'.
Let us, O Lord, make this our Kingdom of God motto, and live and work it out to the best of our abilities.
We give you thanks for this perception and understanding.
O Lord, people matter! Praise eternally is yours!

200.   LUKE 6, vv27,28
Lord, sometimes your children share good things, sometimes evil. When sharing an evil thing, help us to be positive in the sense of opposing it firmly, and constructive in the sense of showing the way forward to something good, so that those with whom we are sharing the evil may be loved; and may we also support them and our efforts with prayer. Praised be your Name! Alleluia!

201.   THE GIFT OF TODAY!
Almighty God,
we thank you for the gift of today:
may we love the day in its entirety.
We thank you for the amazing gift of today:
may we illumine the day as you would have us do.
We thank you for the most excellent gift of today:
may we live the day constructively for all.
Alleluia! Alleluia! Alleluia!

202.   THE GIFT OF LIFE
Almighty God,
I have received the gift of life:
may I appreciate it properly at all times;

may I imbue it with the rational pursuit of love and service, truth and witness;
and may I offer daily thanks for such a precious thing.
Alleluia!

203.   BENIGN KING – a hymn of praise
Benign King, we praise you,
The red sun horizon low,
Perfect orb, we honour you,
To all you mercy show.

Gracious Lord, we adore you,
The black cloud silver lined,
Flaming radiance, we exalt you,
Our darkness by you illumined.

Universal Maker, we bless you,
Grey wisps a subtle lace,
Great luminary we love you,
To all you show your face!

THREE VARIATIONS
204.   YOUR KINGDOM BE!
LORD, help me to be
a raindrop of your truth,
a sunbeam of your love,
a zephyr of your blessing,
though clouds are looming,
this day and every day!

205.   WINSOME WEATHER!
Heavenly Father, help us,
Though cloud is abounding,

To be raindrops of your truth,
Sunrays of your warmth,
Zephyrs of your bounty,
This day and everyday.

206.	to be a RAY!
gRAYcious God, help me
not to stRAY, but rather
to be a RAY of your friendship,
a RAYndrop of your truth,
a zephyRAY of your blessing,
todRAY and everydRAY! Alleluia!

207.	GOD ALL ABOUT US
Lord, we thank and praise you that the natural world about us clothes your most Holy Spirit. When we meet and address it we meet and address you! May we respond appropriately!

208.	WONDERFUL WORLD!
Almighty God, I thank you for your wonderful world, in particular Brother Sun, who gives his light and warmth generously to all. Alleluia!

209.	JOHN 4, VERSE 24 PLUS!
Heavenly Father, you are Spirit and Material, and we worship you in Spirit and Material. Alleluia!

210.	GOD IN ALL REALITY
Heavenly Father, you are in all Reality, spiritual and material, and we worship you in all Reality, spiritual and material. Alleluia!

211.   A BREASTPLATE AGAINST TEMPTATION
Heavenly Father, I am sorry for the sins I have committed in the past;
I am sorry for the sins I am being tempted to commit now, and to which
to a degree I am succumbing;
and I am sorry for the sins I shall commit in the future.
Heavenly Father, please help me.

212.   ANOTHER BREASTPLATE
Heavenly Father, cherish me,
that in your love I may recognise this temptation;
Heavenly Lord, be with me,
that in your fasting I may bear this temptation;
Heavenly Spirit, strengthen me,
that in your power I may overcome this temptation,
and in overcoming may remain in you and for you.

Either prayer (or both) to be repeated while the temptation is carrying out its assault.

213.   GOD BETWEEN SELF AND A BELOVED
Author of all love,
With friendliness imbue me,
Positive, pertinent, pacific,
Refresh us profoundly.

Example of true love,
With caring empower me,
Holding, helping, healing,
Embrace us handsomely.

Spirit of strong love,
With tenderness suffuse me,
Alive, attentive, ardent,
Nurture us abundantly.

These verses and the hymn above, 'Benign King', were based on experiences of the sun and of the spirit.

214. LET US LIVE!

Help us, O Lord, to play our part in achieving the goals we have, to this end doing what is necessary, to this end thinking and working sensibly in a good spirit. Let us live!

215. A PRAYER OF CLEAVING

'Our lover desires indeed that our soul should cleave to him with all its might, and ever hold on to his goodness. Beyond our power to imagine does this most please God, and speed the soul on its course.'

'Revelations of Divine Love'

The original title for the following prayer was a 'A Prayer for Cleansing', but I think in fact it was more a prayer of cleaving.

Lord, cleanse my mind and my tongue, which is an expression of my mind, cleanse my body and my sexuality, which is an expression of my body, cleanse my emotions and my spirit, that I may be released from all tensions and stresses. And may I be given fresh insight and sense of direction, and thus be restored to a sound, peaceful and harmonious condition within. Alleluia!

216. 'WONDERFUL FRIENDLINESS'

Grant me, O Lord, new insight and understanding that I may have more clearly conceived and broadly-based goals.

The title of this prayer also comes from R.D.L. There is hindsight in this and the previous prayer, in that the requests for insight, understanding and sense of direction are based on what had already been given.

217.   A PRAYER TO LOVE GOD (1)
Help me, O Lord, to rest and live in the love you have for me, and to try to love you as I ought; help me also to help others to rest and live in your love and to try to love you appropriately.

218.   A PRAYER TO LOVE GOD (2)
Almighty God, pour down your blessings upon us and help us to live and work for you, to conduct our relationships suitably in the light of your presence within us and without, and to craft our work so that it is fit to be offered to you as a gift. Alleluia!

219.   LOVE THE MOTIVE, LOVE THE CRITERION
Almighty God, help me to love you, your children and your world, to this end making love my criterion and motive in everything all the while.

220.   I THANK YOU, LORD
For dawn alarm of 'titpecker' knocking,
Alert blue tits their round door chamfering,
Within a soft nest on soft mud teasing,
I thank you, Lord.

For Springtime alarm of snowdrops bowing,
Laid-low daffodils the sun restoring,
Red starshells and red coronets glowing,
I thank you, Lord.

For telephone alarm brightly ringing,
Brother's call to healthy holidaying,
To a fine sea by fine sands despatching,
I thank you, Lord.

221. EASTER

For Easter alarm of snowdrops praying,
Spiked coronets and dark pansies bleeding,
Laid-low daffodils the sun resurrecting,
I thank you, Lord.

222. A RESOLUTION

However you treat me, Lord,
however the people I know treat me,
I will press on with being a friend to all,
with trying to be warm, friendly and helpful
both towards yourself and my neightbour,
that is, with loving you.
It won't be easy, Lord, but I will try.
Incidentally, thank you for supporting the idea
of loving you, and of being loving towards the people in my life.
It isn't an easy idea to get a hold on,
and easily side-lined in the press of life. Thankyou, Lord.

223. TO LOVE GOD

Lord, help me to love you:
help me to try to please you in the choices I make with regard to what I do and do not do, and in the manner I do the things I actually undertake;
help me to have a sensitive regard for the traffic of my mind, to keep it pure and where I fail to be sorry to you;
and help me to be clear in my utterances, eschewing communication by inference and hints, which is not fair to the listener, who does not know for sure what I am trying to say.

224. TO BE LOVING

Lord, help me to remember to be loving and kind and gracious ... at all times, and in all situations. Alleluia!

225. CONTENTMENT

Lord, you prevail,
if not in this life in the next you prevail,
your love, your judgement, your justice prevails;
I do not know how this obtains,
but in that it does I am contented. Alleluia!

Written after reading 'Contentment' by John Bunyan.

FOUR PRAYERS ON THE SPIRIT'S OCCUPANCY

During the night I remembered two incidents in which people seemed to manifest a spirit of evil. One incident was on the London Underground when a man opposite me injected himself in the arm. Afterwards it seemed to me that, as he looked around, an evil spirit glittered in his eyes. It occured to me that I would sooner be occupied by the Spirit of Jesus than an evil spirit.

During the afternoon I realised that we are all vessels of the Holy Spirit. This seems contradicted by the remarks above, but only apparently so. The Holy Spirit is still there, since the Spirit is in and around all of us.

226. THE OCCUPANCY OF THE SPIRIT (A)

Lord, I thank and praise you for occupying me with your most Holy Spirit, my mind, my heart, my soul and my body. Let me not say or do anything which is in any way disharmonious with your Holy Spirit, but rather see each, my mind, my heart, my soul and my body, as a means by which to express the Spirit which occupies them. Alleluia!

227. THE OCCUPANCY OF THE SPIRIT (B)

Lord, I thank and praise you for occupying me with your most Holy Spirit, my mind, my heart and my body, and especially do I thank you for revealing to me thereby their true nature. Thankyou, Lord.

228.   FOR THE OCCUPANCY OF THE SPIRIT
Lord, I pray that you, rather than evil spirit, will occupy me within. May I not say, think or do anything which is not in keeping with your Holy Spirit, but rather seek to express It in my daily life, body, heart, mind and soul.

229.   FOR THE OCCUPANCY OF THE HOLY SPIRIT
Lord, I pray that, rather than an evil spirit, you will occupy me with the blessedness of your most Holy Spirit. Inspire and direct the use of all my parts, so that this blessedness is honoured and adored in all my worship and in all my doings. Alleluia!

230.   A THANKSGIVING
Lord, I thank and praise you that your children are vessels of your most Holy Spirit. Help me to behave towards each and every one of them suitably in the light of this wonderful fact.

231.   TO BE INSTRUMENTS
Lord, I thank and praise you that we are vessels of your most Holy Spirit. Help us also to be instruments of this same Spirit in all our doings one with another.

232.   TO SERVE LOVE
Father, you are a God of love. Let all our doings express and serve your purposes and love in relation to all those with whom we have to do this day and for evermore.

233.   TO THE BEST OF MY ABILITY
Gracious Spirit, help me to love everyone to the best of my ability; Gracious Agape, help me to act as far as possible for their good; Gracious God!

234.   THE GOOD OF ALL
Holy Agape, help me, please, at all times to try to will the good of all to the best of my thinking and abilities.

235.   THE WILL OF GOD
Almighty God, I pray that I may do your will; please teach me how I may do it in all matters.

236.   FOUR INVOCATIONS
ONE
Arise, gentle Spirit,
My soul address,
Arise, sweet Spirit,
My soul impress.

TWO
Enter, delicate Spirit,
In heavenly Love be known,
Enter, infusing Spirit,
In Tenderness be shown.

THREE
Awake, sensitive Spirit,
In Life pulsating,
Awake, nurturing Spirit,
In Love Self-giving.

FOUR
Come, holy Spirit,
That which is best;
Come, kindly Spirit,
Be manifest!

237.   LIVING OUT THE SPIRIT
Almighty God, please support me in incarnating your Spirit, and in struggling to live out rationally its qualities in my everyday conduct. Alleluia!

238.   GOD OPERATES, WE CO-OPERATE
Almighty God please operate within me that I may incarnate your Spirit, and help me to co-operate with it by struggling to live out rationally its many wonderful qualities in relation to all your children, including myself. Alleluia!

239.   GOD ADORED AS OUR JUDGE
I adore you as the God who knows all the facts about each and every one of us, whose judgement is reasonably and fairly based on those facts, and whose justice is that of a God of love, fair, decent and honourable. Alleluia!

240.   GOD ADORED AS OUR CREATOR
I adore you as the the creator of life, by long evolutionary development; I adore you as the creator of death, which facilitates that same evolutionary development. Were it the case that the early and late stages of birth and death were wholly benign.

241.   TEACH ME
Lord, teach me to adore you as you would be adored.

242.   GOD EVERYWHERE
Lord, I adore you for being both without us and within us.

243. CO-OPERATORS
Lord, I adore you for being creative, and that we might be co-operators in your creativity and bring new beings, new forms, to life.

244. THE AGAPE GOD
I worship and adore you as the God who acts for the good of each of us, both when you propose and when you oppose; I worship and adore you as the agape God! Alleluia!

245. WITHIN EVERYBODY!
Lord, I am sorry for not recognising 'that of God', neither within myself nor within others. You are within everybody! Alleluia!

246. PERFECT FORGIVENESS
'Perfect forgiveness enables perfect love;
perfect love entails perfect forgiveness.'
Lord, help us to love and forgive each other;
Lord, help us to love and forgive ourselves;
And Lord, help us to love and forgive you.

247. ALL MY WRONGDOINGS
Lord, I am sorry for all my wrongdoings, all my wrongdoings, those where I have done what I should not have done, and those where I have not done what I should have done, for by these wrongdoings I have done real harm, real hurt, and in doing so I have crucified you. I am sorry, very sorry, for all my wrongdoings.

248. ALWAYS IN GOD'S ENVIRONMENT!
Lord, I thank you for the kingdom of God, for it means that I am always in a constructive environment, an environment in which I matter; and one in which I may be the recipient of your SURPRISES!

YOUR EXPRESSIONS OF THE SPIRIT! It is an environment in which you protect me against that which is harmful, and in which I am well regarded and in which I am safe and secure. Praise be to you, O Lord!

249. FOREVER A CITIZEN
Lord, I thank and praise you that I am in your kingdom, that I am a citizen in your kingdom, and must forever remain so. Alleluia!

250. OINTMENT OF THE SPIRIT
Lord, I praise and thank you that I have the ointment of the Holy Spirit within me. Help me to be this ointment in all my doings. Thus may I be your child, both in name and in deeds!

251. KEEPING IN LINE
Lord, in all my thinking and doing help me to conduct myself harmoniously with your spirit, that in doing so I may love and serve you and your children today and forever.

252. THE GOOD OF YOUR CHILDREN
Lord, help me to imitate you, the God of love, to express in my daily conduct and work your sorts of love. When proposing or opposing in any matter may I do so for the good of your children, each and every one.

253. THE SPIRIT OF PEACE
Lord God, by your spirit overcome in me all anxiety and worry in connection with any matter. I praise and thank you, Lord, for dispelling such from the inward man. Alleluia!

254. GRACE
Lord, keep us in your grace; and help us to live it out in our daily lives.

255. HIDDEN EVILS
Lord, show us clearly the evils in our lives, both those we recognise and those we do not recognise, and help us to oppose them and to replace them with your good things. Alleluia!

256. A GENERAL BLESSING
Lord, I hold up to you all those for whom I pray, and all those whom I shall meet on the road of life today, and myself, and ask that you will bless and keep us each and every one.

257. THE SPIRIT OF LOVING-KINDNESS
Lord God, I adore you as an eternal being, whose nature is one of loving-kindness. Alleluia! Alleluia!

258. WITH US
Lord, I thank you that you are with us at all times, bad as well as good. May the everyday happenings of our lives serve your purposes.

259. BE ANXIOUS FOR NOTHING
Lord, I am sorry for worrying, for being anxious. These states are evidently evil, since they have a deleterious effect upon the mind, the body and the soul. Lord, I thank and praise you that you can cleanse us of worry and anxiety and their hurt. Praise be!

260. NOT ANXIETY, BUT PEACE
Lord God, help us to leave worry and anxiety behind, seeing these for

the evils which they are. Grant us your spirit of peace and peacefulness I beseech you. Alleluia!

261. AN EXPRESSION OF CHRISTIAN JOY
Lord, I thank and praise you for your existence! Alleluia!

I said the above prayer having prayed as follows: 'Lord, I praise and thank you for Christian "joy"; grant me experience of this joy, grant me to know this joy, to know in what it consists.' A connection? Surely, for Christian joy could be the joy we have in the Spirit!

262. NEW PEOPLE, NEW LIVES
Lord, I praise and thank you for the wheel of life, for the succession of generations it entails.

263. FOR LOVE
Lord, I praise and thank you for love.

264. FOR THE TRUE FRUIT
Lord, I praise and thank you for the fruit of the Spirit.

265. FOR JOY IN GOD
Lord, I praise and thank you for joy, in particular the joy we have in you, as architect, as incarnated in your children, as ubiquitous spirit! Lord, I praise and thank you for joy in you! Alleluia!

266. FOR JOY AS A FRUIT OF THE SPIRIT
Lord, I praise and thank you for the joy which is the fruit of the Spirit, which is the joy we have in you, the joy of knowing that you are! Alleluia!

267. FOR THE TRUE REALITY
Lord, help me to accept the reality of my everyday life, and to live your Reality in relation to both it and your good Self.

268. TO POINT TO GOD
Lord, I hold up to you my work and ask your blessing upon it. Help me to point to you, and to do so in such ways that you are praised, your world is appreciated and your children upheld.

269. RATHER RATIONALLY CHOSEN LOVE AND SERVICE
Lord, I praise and thank you for your constant presence, and pray that you will help me to love and serve you. However, I have learnt not to expect your constant direction. Rather I must order my love and service by suitable consideration and choice regarding the activities I pursue and the conduct I adopt. Rational love! Rational service! Alleluia!

270. SWEETEN ME!
Lord, by your holy Spirit, sweeten me!

271. HEAL ME!
Lord, by your holy Spirit, heal me!

272. 'FLOWERS OF EARTH AND BUDS OF HEAVEN'
Lord, may the flowers of your most Holy Spirit blossom and bloom in my daily life; and may these same flowers become heavenly fruit. This I ask in your name.

273. TO BE A FLOWER OF THE SPIRIT
Lord, may I be a flower of your most holy Spirit. Please, Lord, please!

274. FOR MERCY
O Breaker of men, have mercy on me;
O Breaker of men's hearts, have mercy on me;
O Breaker of men, have mercy on me!

275. SHOW ME THE WAY
Lord, you have shown me the nature of the work which you wish me to do for you, which is to point to you. Show me the particular ways in which you want me to do this, and how each particular way may be worked out. Grant me your life, and thus show me the ways forward in my work for you!

276. TOUCH OUR HEARTS
Lord, touch our hearts and minds, bodies and souls, with your most holy Spirit, and help us to clothe the words of the Spirit with thought, communication and action, so that your good purposes might be enabled and progressed and your works of love brought to fruition.

277. LORD, BLESS
Lord, bless my heart, may all it loves be blessed;
> bless my eyes, may all they see be blessed;
> bless my hands, may all they do be blessed;
> and, Lord, bless my face, may all your children be blessed in it.

The above prayer is my memory of a prayer heard on Prayer for the Day for 4th June, 1997. I don't think it is the same as the one I heard, but it follows a similar pattern.

278. TO BE A BLESSING
Lord, may I be a blessing in my being,
Lord, may I be a blessing in my doings,
To you, to my neighbour and to myself,
Each hour, each day and for evermore.

As well as remembering the prayer 'Lord, Bless' from Prayer for the Day I thought that this is my role in life, TO BLESS, like the sun to be and to radiate that which blesses, that which brings good to man.

279.   TRUE LIFE
Lord, I adore you as the true life,
by the expression of which you vivify,
you renew, you uphold,
by the expression of which you reveal
your kingdom, your will,
your way forward.
Lord, I adore you as the true life,
As the true life, Lord, I adore you!
Lovely Lord! True life! True, true life!

280.   I MATTER
Lord, I thank you for helping me to see that I matter, that I am a piece of your jig-saw of love.

281.   A PRAYER OF PENITENCE
Lord, I am sorry for thinking, saying and doing those things which are against love, love of you, love of my neighbour and love of myself.

282.   PRIVATE WORSHIP
Lord, I praise and thank you for private worship,
for the opportunity it gives to receive your love for us,
and to learn to be more appreciative of and responsive to your love;
and for the opportunity it gives to express our love for you,
and to learn to love you more and better each and every day. Alleluia!

Worship: an exchange of love between the One worshipped and the worshipper. This prayer proved to be particularly apposite for, during private worship the week following when I was on a painting week in Wales, I learned that the stuff of my religious quest is the Holy Spirit, rather than concepts and precepts.

283.   TO BE A BLESSING (B)
Lord, may I be a blessing in my being,
For you, for myself and for my neighbour;
Lord, may I be a blessing in my doing,
For you, for myself and for my neighbour,
This hour, this day and for evermore.

284.   SUNSHINE OF THE SPIRIT
Lord, help me to be a sun of the Spirit, and to express in my daily life the sunshine of the Spirit! Alleluia!

285.   SUN OF THE SPIRIT
Lord, fuel and re-fuel me that I may be a sun of the Spirit, and express in my daily life the light and warmth of the Spirit. Alleluia.

286.   CLOTHE ME!
Lord, clothe me within with your most Holy Spirit, that I may show forth the fashion of the Spirit. Alleluia!

287.   ORB WEB!
Lord, may I be an orb web, large and round, that I may catch the things of the Holy Spirit, and ingest them!

288.   THE TRUE STUFF, THE REAL STUFF
Lord, I adore you as the true stuff, the real stuff,

which stuff is your Spirit, your most holy Spirit! Alleluia!
Lord, your kingdom is the kingdom of the true stuff, the real stuff, which stuff is your Spirit, your most holy Spirit! Alleluia!

289. IN ALL DUE PROCESSES
Lord, I adore you in all your works,
When you are for, and when you are against;
Lord, I adore you in all your works,
In all due processes and the relationships and the activities they entail;
Lord, I adore you in all your works,
Your kingdom come, your will be done:
Lord, I adore you in all your works. Alleluia!

290. FOR NOT TRANSLATING THE WORDS OF THE SPIRIT INTO ACTION
Lord, I am sorry for not fully recognising or accepting wholly the reality of your Spirit and the possibility of your Spirit speaking within me; and I am sorry for not responding suitably to the words of your Spirit when they have actually been expressed within me, indeed for setting aside your Spirit, negating it, reducing it to a thing of no account. I am sorry.

291. FOR BEING UNAFFECTED BY THE SPIRIT'S LEADINGS
Lord, I am sorry that I have not recognised, have not kept in mind, the very present Reality of your most Holy Spirit; and I am sorry that I have not realised, have not accepted, the very present demands which the Reality of your most Holy Spirit entails in terms of my conduct and of my activities. Lord, I am sorry I have neither recognised nor attempted to conform to the Reality of your Spirit, the True Reality!

292. FOR DISREGARDING THE SPIRIT
Lord, I am sorry that I did not recognise the reality of your Spirit,

particularly in its self-expression in my mind, heart and body, and that I did not recognise the reality of your Spirit in that I could have taken account of it in some way, could have acted upon what it seemed to say, at the very least have given the expressions of your Spirit regard and consideration. Lord, I am sorry.

293. TO PUT THE SPIRIT FIRST (1)
Lord, help me to follow the Spirit, in its nature and its expressions, notwithstanding the conduct and attitudes, particularly the contrary ones, of my neighbours. Lord, help me to put you first. Alleluia!

294. TO PUT THE SPIRIT FIRST (2)
Lord, help me to follow the Spirit, in its nature and expressions, notwithstanding the social norms, or what I take to be the social norms, of the society in which I live. Lord, help me to put you first. Alleluia!

295. FOR FAILING TO RECOGNISE AND RESPOND TO THE SPIRIT
Lord, I am sorry I have not recognised your activity in my life, nor have I put to use the light and love which that activity has brought. Lord, I am sorry.

296. TO LIVE OUT THE SPIRIT
Lord, help us to live and to live out your Spirit in relation to all, for we are in your Kingdom, now, today. Alleluia!

297. A PRAYER FOR THE SINGLE PERSON
Lord, I pray that you will show me whether or not you wish me to have a partner. If you do wish me to have a partner, please show me whom. I can think of no preferable way of going forward than doing so in the direction and with the companion of your Spirit's choice. Alleluia!

298. THE WAY OF THE SPIRIT
Lord, your will be done in all matters;
Lord, your will be made known in all matters;
Lord, your will be incarnated in thought, word and deed in all matters.
Alleluia!

This prayer was composed with a consideration of the possibility of marriage in mind.

299. A PRAYER FOR FORGIVENESS
Lord, send down upon me the healing power of your Holy Spirit; show your love for me, your concern for my good, and cleanse me of all those things which erode your Holy Spirit in me: suspicion, lack of being concerned for the good of, unforgivingness and other things. Lord, I beseech you, bless me with the healing power of your Holy Spirit and cleanse me of all those attitudes which erode your Spirit in me.

300. BETWEEN THE SEXES
Lord, your will be done regarding relationships between the sexes, regarding marriage, regarding sexual activity and family building and regarding the extended family. Your will be done, O Lord, your will be done.

301. A THANKSGIVING
Almighty God, I thank you for your mercy, love and grace to me, even to me; and I thank you also for the greatness and wonder and beauty of your creation. Thank you, O God.

302. THE SUNSHINE OF THE SPIRIT
Lord, may I show forth to all the sunshine of your most holy Spirit, wearing for all the smile of that wonderful sunshine. Alleluia!

Lilies

303. BRIDGES
Lord, let us live in love and peace with all. Where there is division, help us seek to build bridges: bridges of respect and reconciliation, bridges of apologising and making amends. Bridges! Lord, let us live in love and peace with all.

304. TO RETURN GOOD FOR EVIL
Lord, when we are met with suspicion, hostility and hatred, help us to return good for evil, so that we may never fall prey to that worst of diseases, evil doings and spirit.

305. TRUE TO THE HEART OF THE UNIVERSE
O God, help us not only to return good for good, but also return good for evil, that in doing so we may remain true to the heart of the universe, the actual reality in everything. Praise be to you, O God.

306. LET US LOVE OURSELVES ALSO
O Lord, let us have a good will towards our neighbours and let us have a good will towards ourselves, indeed, may we practise towards ourselves the good will that you would have us show towards our neighbours. O Lord, let us love our neighbour as ourselves!

307. TRUE PEACE
Lord, I thank you that you grant us the spirit of peace when we are engaged in the work which you have given to us to do, and thereby support us and encourage us to continue in its doing. Thanks be to you, O Lord.

308. A WAY OF PEACE
Lord, I thank you for the encouragement which you give your children to do the work which is harmonious with your will, and I thank you also

for the recent experience given me of the Spirit as peacefulness as I did work of this kind. Thank you, Lord.

309.　FOR PEACE

Lord, please assist me in seeking and working through opportunities for reconciliation with those towards whom I have misbehaved, and thereby promote your peaceable spirit, your peaceable kingdom.

310.　LIFE!

Lord, let us spend our lives
loving you, our neighbour and ourselves,
shining your truth and beauty,
and pointing to your glory! Alleluia!

311.　LORD, YOU KNOW ALL ABOUT ME

Lord, you know all about me,
 all about my past,
 all about my doings,
 all about my misdoings,
 and all about the things I should have done, but did not.
Lord, you know all about me,
 all about my present,
 the facts of the matter in respect to all aspects of my life,
 my hopes and fears,
 my outlook and attitudes,
 and the behaviour of others towards me.
Lord, you know all about me,
 all about the future,
 both short term and long term.
Lord, you know all about me,
 and knowing all about me,
 you use this knowledge,
 not to judge me,

        but to love me, to act for my good.
Lord, you know all about me,
        help me to see, to understand,
        to take seriously
        all matters in my life,
        especially the words of the Spirit in me,
        and to follow you in the way of love,
        and of acting for our good.
Lord, you know all about me,
        I ask only that you speak clearly,
        speak unambiguously,
        for I am a slow-witted person.
Lord, you know all about me. Alleluia!

312. WELCOME THE SPIRIT!

Lord, I am sorry for initially resenting and deploring the activity of your Spirit, rather than welcoming and rejoicing in it, for your words, whether for or against, are words of love, love for me and others through me.

313. WORK MEANS LOVE

Lord, I am sorry for resenting being seen by you just as a worker, for it is by work, by giving time and effort, that I can incarnate your love for your children, transform your love into a useful reality. Alleluia!

314. TO BE CONSTRUCTIVE

Lord, I am sorry where I have not shown kindliness or helpfulness or constructiveness towards you or my neighbours or myself.

315. FOR ALL IMPERFECTIONS

Lord, I am sorry for all my imperfections and for all my wrong-doings in your eyes; in your complete knowledge of me and in your true judgement I am content.

316. AN ARTIST'S THANKS
Lord, I thank and praise you for pastel pencils;
Lord, I thank and praise you for portraiture;
Lord, I thank and praise you for all media and categories of art.
Thankyou, Lord, thankyou! May I appreciate them all!

317. FOR THE PEACEABLE SPIRIT
Lord, please assist me in seeking and working through opportunities for reconciliation with those towards whom I have misbehaved, and thereby give your peaceable spirit opportunities for expression!

318. LORD, TREAT ME!
Lord, I ask only one thing of you: that you treat me in ways which are appropriate to a Holy Spirit!

319. AN EXERCISE
Lord, I exercise contrition
for conduct which was not harmonious with your holy will;
for not implementing opportunities for carrying out your holy will;
and for not seeing that all aspects of life fall within the ambit of your holy will;
Lord, I exercise contrition,
I am sorry and ask for your forgiveness.
Lord, have mercy upon me.

320. A LOVER'S PRAYER
Heavenly Father, bring cleansing to (NAME) and myself that we may each be Holy Spirit love. Being Holy Spirit love may we become one in this love. Thus may (NAME) and myself enjoy the highest form of union. Alleluia!

321.   PRAYER FOR GUIDANCE (I)
Lord, please show me a path forward regarding (--------). May I think about it carefully, choose sensibly and act responsibly. In anticipation, thankyou, Father, thankyou.

322.   PRAYER FOR GUIDANCE (II)
Lord, I pray that you will show me an acceptable way to take regarding (--------). Please unfold appropriate opportunities for taking forward (--------) according to your will.

323.   PRAYER FOR GUIDANCE (III)
Lord, I hold up to you (--------). I pray that you will open a window of opportunity regarding (--------), and that I might act appropriately in relation to it when you do so.
Thankyou, Lord, thankyou.

324.   TRYING TO SEE THE OTHER PERSON'S POINT OF VIEW
Lord, I am going to put myself in the shoes of (----NAME----), in order that I might try to see (----PARTICULAR MATTER----) from (----NAME----'s) point of view. Having done this, I might be better able to conduct my loving of (----NAME----) in the light of the insight and understanding to which the exercise gives rise. If you would care to support me in this exercise, I should be very appreciative. Thankyou, Lord, thankyou.

I wrote this prayer after hearing Dame Edna Everidge interviewed on the radio. Dame Edna spoke of the (I think) Sweden syndrome. In this syndrome you put yourself on the side of the enemy. Lord Archer was quoted as having practised this in some connection. Of course, my prayer is meant for use in relation to anyone, not only people ill-disposed towards us.

325. PERFECT LOVE THE IDEAL

Almighty God, we recognise that searching standard by which light our conduct is judged: perfect love! In all our relationships may we seek to embody and to express perfect love, whatever the particular type of relationship and the particular activity being undertaken. Where we have failed to meet this exacting standard may we be ready to apologise, to try to sort out any problems our conduct has given rise to, and to make amends, in so far as this is possible.

Whatever our imperfections may we continue to seek this ideal, that we might be perfect even as you are perfect and bring in your kingdom on earth, this day and for evermore.

326. BIRTHDAY PRAYER - THE HEAVENLY MODE

Lord, let us think, say and do things for one another in love, in loving ways, this day and forever. Alleluia!

327. THE HEAVENLY MODE PRE-EMPTED (I)

Lord, help us to see ourselves as instruments of redemption for others, to have in mind only their good, their welfare, and their eternal destiny, as vessels of agape, as vehicles of your love. Alleluia!

328. THE HEAVENLY MODE PRE-EMPTED (II)

Heavenly Father, help us to follow your example by being unconditional love to all, and thus walk in your footsteps, walk in your way. Alleluia!

329. FOR FULFILLING MY VOCATION (I)

Almighty God, I thank and praise you for the vocation which you gave me, to point to you. Help me to implement this in my work, verbal, visual and practical. Thankyou, Lord, thankyou!

330. FOR FULFILLING MY VOCATION (II)
Almighty God, I ask that I may point to you in my work: so might I carry-out the vocation you vouchsafed to me in the nineteen sixties. Alleluia!

331. FOR FULFILLING MY VOCATION (III)
Almighty God, I thank and praise you for the vocation you have given me, and for showing me through experience and inspiration that this great task of pointing to you is carried-out through an ongoing series of small tasks. May I have the determination to persevere with the small tasks, and to present their fruits intelligently in viable and valuable contributions to the society in which I live. Alleluia!

332. FOR FULFILLING A VOCATION (I)
Almighty God, I thank and praise you for the vocation (of ----STATE----) to which you have called me. Help me to implement this for you, for your glory, and for your children. Thankyou, Lord, thankyou!

333. FOR FULFILLING A VOCATION (II)
Almighty God, I ask that I might carry-out the vocation which you have vouchsafed to me in my daily work. Alleluia!

334. FOR FULFILLING A VOCATION (III)
Almighty God, I thank and praise you for the vocation you have given me, and for showing me through experience and inspiration that this great task (of ----STATE----) is carried-out through an ongoing series of small tasks. May I have the determination to persevere with the small tasks, and so make a viable and valuable contribution to the society in which I live, and honour you in living-out your gift, my vocation. Alleluia!

335. LOOK RATHER, LISTEN RATHER

While on a visit to St. Gildas Christian Centre in Langport, Somerset, the chaplain for the week, John Vaughan, told us a story about an artist he had visited in hospital. On returning home the artist invited John to see his pictures, which he did and which John reciprocated. The artist expressed the opinion that when picture-making you should look for a long time at the subject and paint for a short. John, he thought, had looked only a little while and then had galloped through his painting.

John extrapolated this notion to prayer. We tend to get on with speaking to God without any preliminary looking and listening. A better strategy would be to look long and hard at the One we are addressing and then speak. We may find that in fact words are redundant!

During the night I made-up the first version of the following prayer. It utilises John's suggestion and also the thoughts I have had recently in Meeting for Worship about listening to God and being listened to by God.

O lovely Lord, you look upon me;
O lovely Lord, I look upon you;
O lovely Lord, you listen to me;
O lovely Lord, I listen to you;
O lovely Lord, you give yourself to me;
O lovely Lord, I give myself to you;
Help me to look upon you, to listen to you, and to give myself to you, this day, this night.

A second version soon followed:
O lovely Lord, you attend to me;
O lovely Lord, I attend to you;
O lovely Lord, you speak to me;
O lovely Lord, I speak to you;
O lovely Lord, you are mine;
O lovely Lord, I am yours;
Help me to attend to you, to speak to you, and to be yours, now and forever more.

336.　　LOVE THE FOUNDATION

In his book 'My Affair with Christianity', Rabbi Lionel Blue speaks of loving Jesus. I found this helpful in that it moves my relationship with Jesus from one which is based on a theological proposition to one which is based on love, or unconditional positive regard, as might be said. Since the end of the seventies I have been uncertain about the status of Jesus - God, or God imbued man above the norm? - and in moving the basis of my relationship with Jesus from this consideration to that of a loving attitude is a step in the right direction. It does not answer the question, but it provides a proper and acceptable way forward. Yes, indeed!

Jesus, I thank you that the foundation of my relationship with you is love, rather than a particular theological proposition or level of scholarship. We can all, as members of the kingdom of everybody, relate to you in love, bringing to that love our particular insights, knowledge and experience. I feel sure that no-one's love for you is unimportant, does not matter to you. Alleluia!

337.　　TRACTOR POWER

While on a Prayer and Painting Retreat at Glenfall House I painted fields which had been harvested, backed by a pine plantation. A strip had already been ploughed in a field in the mid-distance. When I sat down a lorry had gone down the hill and I thought I might include it on the bend in the road, again in the mid-distance. During that session I painted the sky, background and pine plantation. That night, as I lay awake in the small hours I made-up a prayer about tractor power along the lines of the one that follows. Evidently the ploughed strip had made its mark. Next morning I continued my painting. While doing so a tractor appeared and continued to plough the strip already started. It did not do so for long, but in view of my nocturnal thought my interest in it can be imagined. Of course, it was not a lorry that figured for interest in my painting - it had to be the tractor!

Almighty God, by the tractor power of your holy spirit,

plough the earth of our hearts, minds, bodies and souls,
so that being turned-over and the deep-down brought to the surface,
it may by your light and warmth, your wind and rain,
be re-invigorated, be renewed,
today and everyday! Gracious Lord!

338.   COME TO ME, MY LOVER, COME
On my return home from Glenfall House, where I wrote 'Tractor Power', the theme still occupied me:
Come to me, my Lover, come,
plough me deeply, harrow me thoroughly,
expose every molecule
to your sun's light and warmth, to your rains' wet and cold,
and so revitalise me, and so prepare me, your Spirit earth,
to grow your crop of love! Alleluia!

339.   ALWAYS
One evening at Glenfall House Valerie led a writing session. For the first exercise she gave the first words of several lines, which we had to complete, and so in effect write a short poem:
My God is a --- most holy Spirit,
He is always --- present,
With him I --- walk and talk,
He never --- hurts of harms,
He always --- makes positive moves!
At home this became the following prayer:

O God, most holy Spirit,
always present,
always communing.
always harmless,
always blessing. Alleluia!

340.   TO (---NAME---)

It had been suggested at Glenfall House that we give a card to the person we had prayed for during the week. The words I put in the card I made were in the form of the following prayer:

May the Spirit go with you,
guide you and guard you, day by day.

341.   MY TREASURE

Come to me, most holy spirit, the treasure in a field for which a man sells all that he has, come to me and perform an item of your spirit work within me. Come to me, most holy spirit, the treasure in a field for which a man sells all that he has, come to me and perform a work of love within me. Oh, most holy spirit, my treasure in a field, come to me, come! Thankyou, Lord, thankyou. Praise be! Alleluia!

342.   TO LIVE THE SPIRIT

Come to me, the living God, and help me to live rationally and lovingly today, in order that I may conduct myself harmoniously with your most holy spirit, and in all things express the same. Alleluia! Alleluia!

343.   THE PLAYGROUND

Come to me, most holy Spirit, and be a child at play in the playground within me, cartwheel and hopscotch, tag and conker. Come to me, most holy Spirit, and be yourself within me!

344.   SPIRIT MUSIC

A visit to King's Norton Church, Leicestershire, helped to flesh-out the metaphor in the following prayer.

Come to me, my lover, my own one, come! Make a gallery of me in which to play the music of the spirit; make a chancel of me in which to

sing the songs of the spirit.
And when you have played and when you have sung, let me give voice to the spirit music I have heard in all my doings. Come to me, my spirit music maker, come! Praise be, praise be, praise be!

345.   THE PEARL OF GREAT PRICE
Come to me, most holy spirit, the pearl of great price for which a man will sell all that he has in order to buy it, come to me, most holy spirit, come!

346.   THE WILL OF GOD
Lord, keep me from temptation,
the temptation to do, to think and to say
what is not according to your will;
help me rather to do, to think and to say
what is according to your will,
in my work, in my relationships,
in everything!
This I humbly ask of you, Lord.

347.   THE WAY FORWARD
Lord, with regard to my conduct please help me to love my neighbour as myself, and with regard to my work please help me to point to You. Indeed, may all my thoughts, words and deeds be children of your Spirit, children who exhibit your characteristics and show you a proper regard and respect!

348.   PRAYER OF PENITENCE (I)
Lord, I am sorry for, penitent for,
    all my wrongdoings,
    all my imperfections,
    all my failures to act positively,
from your point of view, in your eyes.

Please accept my penitence.

349. PRAYER OF PENITENCE (II)
Lord, I am sorry for all my sins,
      my sins of thought, word and deed,
      my sins of commission and omission,
and I beg your forgiveness and mercy upon me.

350. ALL THINGS (I)
Lord, I am sorry for the things I have done wrong in relation to (--NAME--). May they through the decomposition wrought by your holy Spirit become the compost for the right things I shall do in the future, growing a vibrant, Godly and caring relationship with (----NAME----). Alleluia!

351. ALL THINGS (II)
Lord, I am sorry for all the things I have done wrong in the past. Through the decomposition wrought by your holy Spirit may they become the compost for the right things I shall do in the future.

352. BOTH YOUNG AND OLD
Lord, I praise and thank you for the elderly, for their wisdom and kindness and for their memories and stories;
and, Lord, I praise and thank you for the young, for their single-minded response to 'life' and for their generosity;
for these riches I thank you, Lord: thankyou.

353. IN THE SPIRIT (I)
Lord, help me to live in the spirit of your Spirit for you, for my neighbour and for myself.

354.   IN THE SPIRIT (II)
Lord, help me to live-out your Spirit in me in relation to you and my neighbour, in particular (----NAME(S)----) with regard to (----).

355.   IN THE SPIRIT (III)
Lord, I thank and praise you that each and everyone of us is a citizen of your kingdom; help me to conduct myself towards everybody as citizens of your kingdom. This I ask for your sake and ours.

356.   THANKYOU (I)
Lord, I praise and thankyou for the love of all and goodwill towards men. May we not forget though that these find expression in practical action in relation to particular individuals. I praise and thankyou for the love of all and goodwill towards men!

357.   THANKYOU (II)
Lord, I praise and thank you that you have been my constant companion throughout my whole life. Thankyou, Lord, thankyou.

358.   THANKYOU (III)
Lord, I thank and praise you that you have been my constant companion throughout my life, and that you have responded to my conversation as you have seen fit. I thank you too that you have kept a watchful eye over me, always having my well-being at heart, that in fact I am an apple of your eye! Thankyou, Lord, thankyou.

359.   THANKYOU (IV)
Lord, I thank and praise you that you have been my constant companion throughout my life, and that you have responded to my conversation as you have seen fit, and at all times have kept a watchful eye over me. Thankyou, Lord, thankyou.

360. TO BE THE PERSON GOD HAS IN MIND
Lord, help me to be a thing of beauty where I stand, like a garden horse-chestnut tree.

361. TO BECOME THE PERSON GOD HAS IN MIND (I)
Lord, help me to become, as well as to achieve;
help me to become the person that You have in mind for me to become,
to become that person by what You are and what You do,
and by what I am and what I do. Lord, help me to put my trust in you!

362. TO BECOME THE PERSON GOD HAS IN MIND (II)
Lord, help me to become as well as achieve;
help me to become the person that You have in mind for me to become,
to become that person by what I am and what I do,
and by what You are and what You do! Alleluia!

363. A PRAYER FOR GUIDANCE REGARDING ADORATION
Almighty God, I pray that you will inspire and guide me regarding that aspect of my worship which I know as adoration. May I in this matter, as in all others, give expression to love of you, and perform the task in ways which are pleasing to you.

364. A PRAYER OF ADORATION
Lord, I adore you as the One whose will is to be done.
Lord, I adore you as the One with whom we should try to be co-operative.
Lord, I adore you as the One whose kingdom is to come,
both directly by the operation of your Holy Spirit in ourselves,
and indirectly by the operation of your Holy Spirit in others

and our co-operation with your Holy Spirit. Praise be!

365.   PRAYER OF PENITENCE (III)
Holy Spirit, we are sorry where we have erred against you in any way, shape or form, both directly in relation to yourself, and yourself in others and in ourselves.
Help us to seek to go forward in your ways, the ways of love, both for yourself and for others and for ourselves. Alleluia!

366.   PRAYER OF PENITENCE (IV)
Lord, I am sorry for all my wrongdoings in your sight,
Lord, I am sorry for all my wrongdoings in your sight;
for my failures of courage in personal relationships;
for the low-minded and crude thoughts I have,
which are not worthy of myself, let alone You;
and especially am I sorry for not sorting-out
relationships and situations in my life
where manifestly they need sorting out.
Help me to seek this day and forever the brotherhood of heaven,
where-in reside unity and harmony and love.
Lord, I am sorry for all my wrongdoings in your sight.

367.   PRAYER OF PENITENCE (V)
Mea culpa, mea culpa, mea culpa.

368.   PRAYER OF PENITENCE (VI)
Lord, I am sorry for my sinfulness, have mercy upon me;
Lord, I am sorry for my sinfulness, have mercy upon me;
Lord, I am sorry for my sinfulness, grant me your peace.

369.   FOR HOLY SPIRIT LOVE
Lord, I praise and thank you for (----NAME---'s) holy spirit love, and

especially today do I thank you for its (--------).

370. THANKS FOR PENITENCE – THE BEST FORM OF PRAYER?
Lord, I praise and thank You for penitence,
for being contrite before You,
for saying sorry to You.
And, Lord, I praise and thank You that in this we have
a way back to being welcomed by You,
and a way forward as a member of the family. Alleluia!

While praying this I thought of Rembrandt's drawing of the prodigal son returning home. Do you remember a picture?

371. PUBLISHING FOR GOD
Lord, I hold up to you the possibility of publishing and distributing through the chain of S.P.C.K. bookshops. Please guide me in this matter, and regarding any other way of publishing and distributing my writings. Help me to remember that my work is the nurturing and nourishing of souls, for their well-being and your eternal glory. Alleluia!

372. FOR THE TOUCH OF THE SPIRIT
Lord, touch and fill my mind, my body, my heart and my soul with your love, with your most holy Spirit! Praise be, Lord, praise be!

373. THE LORD'S WILL BE DONE
Lord, your will be done on earth as it is in heaven. May your Spirit guide and govern all aspects of our relationship and the activities we undertake.

374. WONDERFUL STUFF
Lord, I adore you as being

positive, pure, perfect;
Lord, I adore you as being
wholesomeness, health, wholeness;
Lord, I adore you,
sublime in nature, wonderful stuff!
Alleluia!

375.   SPIRIT MUSIC (II)
Lord, I adore you, adore your Spirit music,
its character and its nature,
in particular its purity and power. Alleluia!

376.   PRAYER OF PENITENCE (VII)
Lord, I am sorry that I behave in ways
which do not express your Spirit.
Help me, at all times, and in all places,
in my thinking, doing and speaking, including my worshipping,
to behave in ways which express your Spirit,
and which thereby demonstrate my love for you.

377.   PRAYER OF PENITENCE (VIII)
Lord, help me to be a servant of your Spirit -
an instrument, a tool, hands and feet of your Spirit -
and to remember that in rationally loving my neighbour as myself
I am making of myself such a servant, instrument, tool, hands and feet.
Lord, help me to be a servant of your Spirit.

378.   PRAYER OF PENITENCE (IX)
Lord, help me to order my interior life and my exerior life so that I may
perfectly love you, the living God, my neighbour and myself.

379.   PRAYER OF PENITENCE (X)

Lord, I am sorry for all my sins, especially the sins arising from ignorance and loneliness. With regard to my delusion I see that knowing the will of God is always arrived at rationally, and is demonstrated through my own will, as is my love of you.

380.   GOD'S WILL

Lord, I am sorry for all my wrongdoings. I accept full responsibility for them. In future I shall use my judgement to determine what I think is right. If this appears to mean going against you, in the shape of what I believe to be your 'words', I shall do so. In the past I have given 'authority' to what I believe to be your 'words', which has led to me acquiescing in them, and this in turn has led to some very unhappy situations. It seems to me better to follow my own judgement, even if this means seemingly going against you. I am then fully responsible. I do not think I am superior to your 'words.' It just seems better to act like this, regarding things from a pragmatic point of view. Your 'words' can be put on hold, so to speak, until I can see them to be appropriate by my own judgement. This way I am not rejecting them outright. In the meantime I can do what I think is best, what I think is right, only too aware that I may well be wrong, that I may have failed to recognise some excellent, helpful guidance. For it is true that you always do figure in situations and always do have this on offer. The problem is recognising it, and then determining to follow it in some sensible, practical way.

381.   THANKSGIVING FOR THINGS AS THEY ARE (I)

Lord, I thank and praise you for your heel, for the destructive punishment which you inflict upon your children for their mistakes - mistakes in searching for you, mistakes in loving their neighbour - by means of hidden psychological and social mechanisms. Lord, I am destroyed - almost! Alleuia!

382.   THANKSGIVING FOR THINGS AS THEY ARE (II)

Lord, I thank and praise you for your heel. It almost destroys us, but it also keeps us from getting above ourselves.

383. REALITY
Lord, I adore you in reality.

384. FATHER SPIRIT
Lord, I adore the holiness and beauty of your Father Spirit.

385. LORD, MOST HOLY SPIRIT
Lord, most holy Spirit, help me to rest in You, to rest in Your love;
Lord, most holy Spirit, help me to worship You, to show forth my love for You;
and Lord, most holy Spirit, help me to work for You, to show forth your love for my neighbours and for myself.
Gracious Lord, heavenly King, have mercy upon me. Alleluia!

386. THE LORD'S WILL
Lord, your will be done on earth as it is in heaven. May your Spirit guide and govern what we do in our relationships. May Jesus show us the way forward. Alleluia!

387. A NIGHT PRAYER
Lord, cover me with your Holy Spirit, and by your covering protect me from all evil, evil spirit and evil's temptations;
Lord, cleanse me with your Holy Spirit, and by your cleansing purge me of all evil, evil spirit and evil's temptations;
Lord, comfort me with your Holy Spirit, and by your comforting let me enjoy your beauty, wholesomeness and strength. Alleluia!

388. GOD'S WAYS, NOT MINE

Almighty God, I hold-up to you my conduct, and thank and praise you that I have been lead to reflect that we are too easily satisfied with our own ideas about our conduct, for example, about loving someone, and that rather we should seek your ideas, your inspirations, your opportunities with regard to our conduct in this and in all of life's varied departments. I thank and praise you that having reflected on the way that you have loved me I have seen that in our conduct, in our loving, we should always seek some good for the loved person, and do so in a way full of regard and consideration. Help me to conduct myself in your ways rather than my own, and in doing so seek to imitate you, to try at all times to be like you in spirit and in fact. Praise be!

SOME RHYMING COUPLETS

In the Dorothy Sayers' short stories which feature him, Mr Montague Egg, at critical points in his detective work, is wont to quote from that tool of his trade, 'The Salesman's Handbook'. His detection is purely amateur, since his livelihood is earnt as a commercial traveller in wines and spirits. The handbook evidently includes a collection of rhyming couplets containing the distilled wisdom of those who follow this line of work, and Mr Egg is wont to apply them to his detection as appropriate. When it occurred to me to write some prayers in verse, having just read some of these stories, it was not surprising that I chose the rhyming couplet!

389. FOR GOD'S WAYS (I)

Dear Lord, keep us in your heavenly way,
and let us never in the devil's stray!

The second line reflects the thinking of St. Francis de Sales in the 'The Love of God', Book 11, chapter 21, paragraph 3.

390. FOR GOD'S WAYS (II)

Let my words, Lord, instead of weapons, be

expressions of your Kingdom Love through me!

391.   TO THE SPIRIT IN THE NIGHT-WATCH (I)
By night, my Love, reside and rest in me;
by day, for You, I'll work incessantly!

392.   TO THE SPIRIT IN THE NIGHT-WATCH (II)
Holy Spirit, reside and rest in me,
for I am yours, my true Love, eternally!

393.   TO THE SPIRIT IN THE NIGHT-WATCH (III)
Kingdom of God, in me reside and rest:
With You I'll give for all my very best!

394.   ALWAYS A FRIEND
Almighty God, we thank and praise you that you can only express 'that of God' in relation to us and can therefore never be other than A FRIEND towards us. We thank and praise you for this and rejoice that your dealings with us are always positive, always for the good of others and of ourselves. Alleluia! Praise be!

This prayer is based on the notion that a friend is someone who is currently exhibiting 'that of God' towards us, while an enemy is someone who is not. See the thought 'On Being a Friend'.

395.   THE RIGHT SIDE - GOD'S SIDE!
Lord, we recognise that the dividing line between good and evil runs through each one of us. Help us to seek to keep ourselves on the good side of the divide, on your side of the divide. Help us also to share your suffering when we meet with evil in other people, and to be penitent before you when we put ourselves on the evil side of the divide, by

thinking, speaking and doing that which is in opposition to you. Keep us in your love and in your mercy today and everyday. Yes, Lord!

396. TRUE FRIENDS!

Almighty God, we recognise that the dividing line between Good and evil runs through each and every one of us and that we may give expression in our lives to one or the other. Help us to try to give expression to the Good in us and to try to avoid giving expression to the evil. We also recognise that by giving expression to the Good in us, to that of You in each and everyone of us, we make ourselves friends to all with whom we speak, with all with whom we have any dealings, true friends, whose friendliness is based on the only true Good, that of You! Praise be!

397. A CENTENARIAN'S THANKSGIVING (FOR ALICE)

Lord, I thank you for the gift of life
and the many wonderful attributes it has entailed:
a clear and ready mind;
a keen interest in the people I know, their doings and their well-being;
a continuing concern for what is happening in the world;
and I thank you for the resilience which has enabled me to span a hundred* years!
Thankyou, Lord, thankyou!
*Or our own number of years if we say the prayer for ourselves.

398. MAY I NOT FORGET

Lord, may I not forget that to express your most holy Spirit in the different relationships in my life, in all their various aspects, is always a priority, however tempting behaving in a contrary manner may be. Lord, may I not forget this priority.

Langham Church

399. ALWAYS WITH ME
Lord, I thank and praise you that you always walk with me, are ever at my side; and I thank and praise you that all the words you speak are true, pertinent and helpful. Thankyou for bringing me to appreciate your constant presence and the constant rightness of your words, and help me to trust you and to be guided by what you say, this day and for evermore. Gracious Lord!

400. HOLY UNION
Lord, I thank you for the holy union of a man and a woman, and the mutual protection, provision and procreation it enables. Gracious Lord, holy God.

401. FOR ME
When you are for me, you are for me;
When you are against me, you are for me;
When I am for you, you are for me;
When I am against you, you are for me;
When I am for others, you are for me;
When I am against others, you are for me:
Always for me – lovely Lord!

402. FOR OTHERS
Lord, help me to be for others as you are for me. As you are always for me, help me to be always for others. In this way, Lord, I shall make good my aim to be an upholder of agape in all matters, at all times. Praise be!

This prayer arises from the previous one. God's conduct towards us is always a clue as to what our conduct towards each other should be.

403. THE WAY OF LOVE
Lord, I thank and praise you for the apprehension of Love you gave me

at The Grange in Ellesmere. I also thank and praise you for the notion I had prior to this that Love might be incarnated in our daily lives in loving thoughts, words and deeds. Bearing in mind the shortcomings and wrongdoings of others and myself please show me especially how Love might be implemented in relation to our imperfections. Help me to Love on a personal basis, having regard and respect for each individual in their own right, including myself. I praise and thank you for the apprehension of Love you gave me! Alleluia!

404.   LORD!
Lord, I thank and praise you for being with us and for us at all times!
Lord, in the imitation of your good self, help us to be with and for all your children, including ourselves, at all times!
Thus, Lord, in being your ministering angels, may we create a holy unity, a unity of love, a unity of your Spirit!
Lord, I thank and praise you for being with us and for us at all times!
Praise be!

405.   THE LIVING GOD AND OURSELVES (1)
        Almighty God,
we look forward to your forgiveness,
        who knows all;
to your mercy,
        who loves all;
and to your judgement,
        whose will will be done!
Alleluia!

406.   THE LIVING GOD AND OURSELVES (2)
        Almighty God,
we look for your forgiveness,
        who knows all,
and for your mercy,

who loves all,
and for your words,
> uttered in perfect knowledge and love.
> Alleluia!

407. MIRACLE (1)

Come, Holy Spirit, fill me completely, fill me with your good Self, and in your suffusion I shall be given holiness, the wholeness of love and purity and healthy sexuality.
Come, Holy Spirit, fill me, suffuse me, uphold me! Gracious Spirit, alleluia!

408. MIRACLE (2)

Come, Holy Spirit, fill me, O fill me, suffuse me, O suffuse me, and in your suffusion I shall have wholeness, I shall have fullness of love, of purity and of sexuality. Fill me, O fill me, suffuse me, O suffuse me, gracious Spirit, Holy Spirit! Praise be!

These prayers reflect miracles, that is, the interpenetration of the natural (me!) with the supernatural, the spiritual. This definition of miracle I heard in a Thought for the Day given by Dr. Colin Morris, 14th October, 1999.
Nothing can separate us from this love, the love of God.

409. OVERNIGHT RECHARGING

Come, Holy Ghost, may I be by your side this night: recharge please my inner being with the power which no man can prevent; recharge my mind with the illuminations of your Spirit and the renewed understanding they surely bring; and recharge and refurbish my body with your Spirit love and scintillating life. And so recharged, and so renewed, I shall do the work which you lay upon me through the approaching day, and walk straight and tall in a world which always you seek to bless. Thankyou, Lord, thankyou!

410. TREMENDOUS ENERGIES (1)

Lord God, we thank and praise you for the tremendous energies which inform and make possible our lives: the energies of the air, sometimes in the shape of powerful winds, as presently when they are stripping the trees of their dead and dying leaves; the energies of the sun pouring out light and warmth upon us, and the energies of growth as in the strong, strong growth of plants and trees and their present autumnal preparations for the approaching new year. Lord God, we thank and praise you for these energies and the change and the variety and the sustenance which make possible and enrichen our lives. Thankyou, Lord God, thankyou!

411. TREMENDOUS ENERGIES (2)

Living God, we thank and praise you for the tremendous energies which inform our daily lives: the energies of transformation by which plants and trees change the light and heat of the sun into life-sustaining products, and the energies in all living things of growth and reproduction. We thank and praise you for these tremendous energies, in particular their manifestation in the English countryside, a countryside which is yours and expresses you, and for the opportunities we have to enjoy and to respond to them. Such a tremendous privilege, praise be, living God!

412. LOVING GOD

Lord, help me to love you for yourself;
help me to love you as you.

413. THE GIFT OF ADORATION

Lord, grant me the gift of supernatural love,
the gift of charity,
the gift of the love of yourself,
your good self.

Lord, grant me the gift of the love of you,
this day and every day,
while on earth and forever!

414. EVERY STEP OF THE WAY
O Lord, I adore you, I adore you,
that every step of the way here on earth
is a step with you.
We walk with you,
at all times we walk with you,
at all times we walk in your presence,
living God, holy God.
O Lord, I adore, I adore you! Praise be!

415. THROUGH AND THROUGH
Lord, I adore you as a Spirit whose quality is love through and through, through and through. Alleluia!

God can only love as that is his nature. God loves his children, loves them as they are, just as they are, and WE MUST DO THE SAME!

416. FOR YOUR CHILDREN
Lord, I adore you for being love, for being for your children, for being for your children this day and forever more. Praise be!

417. THIS WORLD GOD'S WORLD
Lord, I adore you as spiritual power
and I adore you that your spiritual power
translates into physical energies,
the physical energies we find in our world.
I adore you that our physical world
manifests you,
is an expression of your very Self,

your Holy Spirit Self!
I adore you, Lord!

THE HOLY PHYSICAL AS WELL AS THE HOLY SPIRIT, SINCE THE PHYSICAL IS A MANIFESTATION OF THE SPIRIT.

418. THE ROMANTIC LOVE OF GOD
Lord, I adore you; I adore you as a Spirit, a Holy Spirit, a Holy Spirit of love. Lord, I adore You; Lovely Lord!

419. TO FORGIVE
Lord, help me to keep to your way of love. To this end help me to forgive the misbehaviour of others towards me, and of myself towards myself.

420. GOD'S WAYS OF LOVE
Lord, help me to seek your ways of love rather than be content with my own. When you show a particular way, help me to progress along it.

421. ALL MY WRONGDOINGS
Lord, I am sorry for all my wrongdoings, in particular my wrongdoing in respect to .... ★★★ ......
A wrongdoing (or wrongdoings) can be itemised here: ...... ★★★ ......

422. ALL MY SINS (I)
Lord, I am sorry for all my sins.
SINS: wrongdoings as God sees them, not as we see them.

423. THAT WE MAY ALSO FORGIVE
Lord, you forgive us all our sins; thankyou! Please help us each and

everyone to recognise our responsibilities in this matter as indicated in the Lord's prayer. Please, Lord, please.

424.   AS YOU LIKE, LORD
Lord, help me to conduct myself, in all areas of life, in ways which you like, in ways which please you. This I beseech you, Lord.

425.   ALL MY SINS (II)
Lord, I am sorry for all my sins. Have mercy upon me.

426.   TO BE INSTRUMENTAL
Lord, help us to be instruments of your light, life and love, to be instruments of your most holy Spirit, for You and for all your children, this day and forever more.

427.   FORGIVE ME, LORD
Lord, I am sorry for all my wrongdoings, both recent ones and those done a longer time ago. Please have mercy upon me, please forgive me. Thankyou, Lord.

428.   ALL
Lord, I am sorry for all of my sins, for all that is past. Lord, I am sorry, have mercy upon me.

429.   THANKSGIVING FOR GOD'S LOVE
Lord, I thank and praise you that I am always the apple of your eye, and that all your words and acts in relation to me have my good at heart. Praise be!

430. EVERYTHING

Lord, I thank and praise You for everything that YOU ARE, for everything that YOU DO and for everything that YOUR WORLD IS! WONDERFUL GOD!

431. IN THE BUBBLES

Lord, I thank and praise you for being the God who bubbles-up within, and who is in the bubbles! Alleluia!

432. THE GOD WITHIN

Lord, I thank and praise you
for being the God whose spirit voice speaks within,
speaks softly within;
for being the God whose spirit power discharges within,
thrusts healingly within;
for being the God whose spirit finger touches within,
enlivens encouragingly within;
and for being the God whose spirit light shines within,
shines within as love!
Lord, I thank and praise you!

433. WONDERFUL INDEED!

Lovely Lord, most Holy Spirit,
I thank and praise You
that the One in whom I reside,
and who resides in me,
is the One in whom I have all things,
and who loves me as their own!
Alleluia! This is wonderful indeed!

434. GOD'S SELF-LIMITATION

Lord, I thank and praise you for your self-limitation in your address to your children, in that you only speak in terms of what has been experienced by the recipient of your word; that you only speak, if no experience has been had in a particular matter, by the Spirit's approval or disapproval in relation to it, by a Spirit 'yes', of a Spirit 'no'.

You recognise the requirement, the need, for each person to experience the material and spiritual worlds in order to know them and relate to them rationally, and that your address to each person must fit in with this requirement, which is to say that you limit yourself in your address to the actual experience of the recipient, even though yours is greater and includes foreknowledge in respect to any current situation and choice.

Lord, I thank and praise you that you do not address a person in terms outside of their experience, that you make yourself as strictly limited by it as they are themselves. Praise be! I thank and praise you for this!

435. GOD'S WALK WITH US

Lord, I thank and praise you for your walk with all those for whom I pray, and for the light, life and love you bring into the lives of each one of us. Alleluia!

436. CONSTANTLY

Almighty God, I praise and thank you for being constantly with me, for being constantly for me, for your nature is pure love, pure unadulterated love! Praise be! Alleluia!

437. ONLY BLESSING

You can only bless, Lord,
Therefore I can only bless!
Yes, Lord! Praise be!

438. BUBBLE WRAPPED

You enfold me in your Spirit, Lord.
How happy are those bubble wrapped so!

Yes, Lord! Praise be!

439.   A-OKAY
You are okay, my Love, A-okay,
Therefore I am okay, A-okay!
Yes, Lord! Praise be!

440.   THE BEST ENCOURAGEMENT
You are the One who wants absolutely the best for me,
Who, when the dark, the depression, is deepest,
'Always strikes the sweetest, the best encouragement.'

The quotation in the last line is from 'The Love of God', Book 11, chapter 21.

441.   THEOREM
You are okay, my Lord,
therefore I am okay.
Alleluia! Praise be!

442.   THE VOICE OF LOVE
Your voice, Lord, is the voice of love.
Help me to hear your voice and having heard it to follow it.
Help me also to be your voice of love in my daily life.
Thankyou, Lord, thankyou.

443.   CARE FOR ALL
Lord, help me to care for your children, for their own sakes and since in caring for them I care for you. Praise be to you, O Lord.

444. THE PURE GOLD OF CHARITY

Lord God, grant me a ceaseless desire for the pure gold of charity, the root from which all blessings spring; grant that I may truly desire to care for you, the source of life, where I can drink deeply of your favour; and grant that I may truly desire to care for my neighbours in all their infinite variety! Alleluia!

The above prayer is based on The Love of God, book twelve, chapter 2, paragraph 5.

445. BUILDING THE KINGDOM

Lord, I pray that you will guide me with regard to building your lovely Kingdom here of earth. Lord, grant me your guidance. Praise be!

446. BUILDING THE CITY

Lord, pour down your light, life and love with regard to building your wonderful City here in our wonderful country. Open my eyes that I may see the way forward for me in regard to this wonderful project! Alleluia!

447. LORD, CLEANSE ME!

Lord, cleanse me of all that is not of you, cleanse me of all that is not of your Holy Spirit! Lord, cleanse me, cleanse me, O cleanse me!

448. ALWAYS SHINING (1)

Lord, I thank and praise you for the radiant sun, which, however cloudy the skies, always shines; and I thank and praise you for your spiritual sun, which, whatever the problematic relationships and situations we may have, also always shines. Praise be! Alleluia!

449. ALWAYS SHINING (2)

Lord, I thank and praise you that you always shine whatever our personal situations, just as your glorious sun always shines whatever the climatic conditions. Help us to make the best of both for the good of all. Praise be!

450.   ALWAYS SHINING (3)
Lord, your physical sun shines always whatever the climatic conditions of the area we live in, and your spiritual sun shines always whatever the personal conditions which presently obtain in our lives. O Lord, we thank and praise you for the constant shining of your two suns! Alleluia! Praise be!

451.   AS IN HEAVEN (1)
Heavenly Father, we thank and praise you for your holy Spirit. By the power of that same Spirit fill our hearts with your love, invest our minds with truth, and strengthen our wills so that we might try to conduct ourselves at all times according to your will! So may your kingdom come on earth as your kingdom is in heaven! Alleluia!

Recently I attended a memorial service. During his contribution the priest spoke of love in the heart, truth in the mind and strength of the will. I felt this was a very neat encapsulation of the religious life.

452.   AS IN HEAVEN (2)
Lord, let love fill my heart,
truth guide my mind,
and strength attend my will,
that your will and work may be done
here on earth as they are in heaven!
Praise be!

453.   O LORD, FILL ME
O Lord, fill me with your Love, that that Love might show me the way forward in all aspects of my life. Fill me to overflowing with your most holy Spirit, the Spirit of your most holy Love, that all your children

might be properly loved by me in harmony with your will. Alleluia, Lord, alleluia!

454. OUR BEING

This morning I spent a part of my devotional period thanking God for his being. While having my breakfast I listened to Radio 4, on which the Bishop of Oxford, Richard Harries, gave Thought for the Day. In the context of the recent concern over eating disorder problems he spoke about body image. He recalled how, as a teenager, he had been concerned about having too long, too thin legs, but that his concern had been ameliorated by discovering that one of his Forrester heroes suffered from the same problem! He concluded by suggesting that we should aspire to a positive attitude towards ourselves. We should seek to bless what we are, as we are, and be thankful for our being. After breakfast, while washing, the connection between my prayer and the Bishop's thought occurred to me, and I interuppted my activity to write the following prayer.

Thank you, Lord, for being, your being and my being. Help me to appreciate and to be thankful for our beings, and to bless them as they are. Thank you, Lord, for being, both yours and mine. Alleluia!

455. PRAYER IS ALWAYS GOOD

Almighty God, we thank and praise you that you redeem our prayers by always bringing good out of them. However, incomplete, mistaken or ill-judged they might be you always, by your response, bring good into the situation to which they relate. We cannot forecast your activity, it will doubtless be entirely different to any expectations we might have, but we thank and praise you that it will be beneficial to ourselves and those for whom we pray. Thank you, Lord, for redeeming our prayers by always bringing good out of them. Praise be! Thank you, Lord!

456. THANKS FOR THE GIFT OF SIGHT

Lord, I praise and thank you for the gift of sight, for the wonderful way our world is made real to us by complex and subtle biological mechanisms, and I praise and thank you for the pleasure, excitement and playfulness to which this amazing gift can give rise. Thank you, Lord, thank you. Praise be!

457. LORD, HAVE MERCY (1)

Lord, we live in you and you in us. Anything we think, do or say is done in relation to you. Have mercy upon us!
Some of these things are offensive and unacceptable to you. Have mercy upon us!
Please forgive us the imperfections which we hourly inflict upon you. Have mercy upon us!
Help us to seek a higher plane, the plane of the Spirit. Lord, have mercy upon us, have mercy upon us!

Perhaps we need a word of comfort:
When I did fall
I mercy found,
Betwixt the stirrup
And the ground.
Some believe that MERCY has the last word. This quote from a tomb stone I heard on a Thought for the Day given by the Bishop of Southwark, Thomas Butler.

458. WONDROUS REALITY, FACTUAL REALITY

Gracious Lord, help us to submit ourselves to you as wondrous reality, and with the passage of time to get to know you better and better through daily, mutual communion, get to know you 'experimentally' as Friends were once wont to say. Let us not make you in our own images, but rather humbly learn about you and how to love you, as you actually, factually are! Gracious Lord, help us to submit ourselves to you as wondrous reality, factual reality. Alleluia! Praise be! Gracious Lord!

459. WORKING FOR GOD

Almighty God, guide us in the work that you would have us do for you, for our neighbour and for ourselves. Not only may we do the work that you would have us do, but also do it for the purposes and in the ways which are pleasing to you. May the work that we do be of benefit to our neighbour and to ourselves today and everyday. Praise be! Praise be!

460. WHAT A WONDERFUL WORLD!

Almighty God, we thank and praise you that we each have an inner self which is more precious than rubies. Help us to recognise and rejoice in this hidden, valuable self in one another, thus bringing to ourselves an abundance of happiness and well-being and contentment. How wonderful it is to recognise and value unique hidden beings going about their activities in their individual and precious ways. What singers, what songs! Almighty God, we thank and praise you for such wonders! Alleluia!

The above prayer owes something to the experience of a concert given earlier in the week by the choir in which I sing.

461. HOLY SPIRIT (1)

Lord, may your Spirit love be whole within me, and may that Spirit love direct the course of my life.

462. HOLY SPIRIT (2)

Lord, may your Holy Spirit be whole within me, and may your Holy Spirit direct the course of my life.

463. HOLY LOVE (1)

Lord, may your holy love make me whole and direct the course of the rest of my life.

464. HOLY LOVE (2)
Lord, may your holy love fill me and make me whole, and may my wholeness direct the course of my life

465. THE FAITHFUL ONE
Lord, I adore you as the true one, the faithful one, for you are ever present, ever ready in your Spirit-speak to generate pertinent, constructive input. Thank you, Lord, thank you.

466. THE POWERFUL ONE
Lord, I adore you as a God of infinite power. Lord, I adore you as a God of infinite control over your power, so that it is always quantitatively appropriate for the work you have determined to do. Praise be!

467. LORD, I ADORE YOU (1)
Lord, I adore you, I adore you,
I adore you as love, as designer,
as designer of every kind of love,
caring love, sexual love, family love,
friendship love, God love.
Lord, I adore you, I adore you as love,
as designer! I adore you! Alleluia!

The seven wonders of the living God: love, truth, beauty, presence, pertinence, intelligence and wisdom. There can be others, of course!

468. LORD, YOU ARE THE TRUTH
Lord, you are truth, and I adore you as truth;
Lord, you are truth, and in you all that is actually so coheres;
Lord, you are truth, and I adore you as truth. Praise be!

469. PRAYER OF ADORATION (1)
Lord, I adore you, Lord, I adore you...
(over and over freely, interpolating freely as follows)
as the living God...
as the eternal God...
eternal spatially... eternal temporally...
as the loving God, which is eternal also...
Lord, I adore you, Lord, I adore you!

470. PRAYER OF ADORATION (2)
Lord, I adore you, Lord, I adore you,
as the living God,
as the author of life,
as the author of life's richness, and of its continuity.

Lord, I adore you, Lord, I adore you,
as the eternal God,
eternal in time, eternal in space,
eternal in being, oh yes, Lord, eternal in being.

Lord, I adore you, Lord, I adore you,
as the loving God,
whose very nature is love,
who expresses love and can only express love.

Lord, I adore you, Lord, I adore you!
O praise be! O Lord! Amen, amen, amen!
Alleluia, alleluia, alleluia! Praise be!

471. LORD, I ADORE YOU (2)
Lord, I adore you; teach me how to adore you.

472.　GOD ENDURES

Lord, I adore you for who you are and I adore you that you endure, that as you were yesterday so you are today, that as you are today so you will be tomorrow. Lord, I adore you for who you are and that you endure. Praise be!

473.　GOD GOES ON

Lord, I adore you: I adore you that you are, I adore you that you are who and what you are, and I adore you that who and what you are go on, today, tomorrow and after tomorrow. Lord, I adore you! Lord, I adore you!

474.　GOD'S BEAUTY

Lord, I adore you;
Lord, I adore you in your beauty;
Lord, I adore you in the beauty of your Spirit;
and, Lord, I adore you in the beauty of the clothing of your Spirit.
Lord, I adore you in your beauty!
Alleluia! Praise be!

475.　FOR CLEANSING

O Lord, the God who is love, let your love cleanse my soul and my body now and forever.

476.　ALL THAT IS NOT OF YOU

O Lord, cleanse me of all that is not of you, not of your most holy Spirit. Cleanse me of all spiritual poison, all moral pus, that you may be able to like me, and that I may be honourable in the eyes of my neighbour and clean in my own. O Lord, cleanse me, please cleanse me.

477.   I AM SORRY
Lord, I am sorry for all my sins, all my offences against you.

478.   CLEANSE ME
Lord, cleanse me of all that is not of your Spirit, of anxiety and worry, of resentment and discontent, and of lust.
Fill me with your precious Spirit, with your precious ointment, love, with your peace and harmony, with your steadiness and acceptance, and with your desire.
Lord, heavenly King, take pity upon me, have mercy upon me. Cleanse me, O cleanse me! Fill me, O fill me! Gracious Lord!

479.   FOR WHOLENESS
Lord, make me whole in your love, and to this end cleanse me by your Spirit. Thank you, Lord, thank you.

480.   MADE WHOLE!
Lord, may I incarnate your most holy Spirit, and in incarnating your most holy Spirit may I be made holy, may I be made whole! Praise be to you, O Lord, forever more!

481.   THE THINGS OF THE SPIRIT
Lord, may I incarnate your most holy Spirit, and the good things of your holy Spirit, such as......... Praise be!

482.   LORD, I AM SORRY (1)
Lord, I am sorry for all my sins,
all the thoughts, words, deeds, which are wrong in your sight, which I have committed.
Lord, I am sorry for all my sins,

please forgive me, please help me to forgive others their sins, please forgive me. Lord, I am sorry for all my sins. Lord, I am yours forever.

483. LORD, I AM SORRY (2)

Lord, I am sorry for being a force against you,
for being a force against one of your goods;
for not being a force of you and for you,
for not being a force of and for one of your goods.
Lord, I am sorry, please forgive me,
have mercy upon me, have mercy upon me.

484. REGARDING BITTERNESS

Lord, I am sorry for any bitterness in my heart towards anyone. Let me be an instrument of your good things to everyone!

485. REGARDING DEVIOUSNESS

Lord, I am sorry for any deviousness in my heart in relation to anyone. Help me to be open with everyone.
(Deviousness arises in relation to the things which we hide from each other.)

486. REGARDING SUSPICION

Lord, I am sorry for any suspicion in my heart regarding anyone. Let perfect love for all cast out suspicion!

It is good to be aware of our own imperfections, for this awareness makes possible confession and penitence, and the possibility of correcting our own conduct. However, the imperfections of others may not be seen as excuses for the practice of our own, even in our hearts.
It is our aim in life to live out God's love, to bless. It is in the context of this aim that confession and penitence take place.
Evil is reduced by our loving and by our being cleansed.

487.   FOR LOVE (1)

Lord, help me to live for your kingdom of love and to this end cleanse me of all that does not belong to your kingdom. Lord, I rest in you, for you; help me to bring-in your kingdom of love this day and every day. Praise be!

488.   FOR LOVE (2)

Lord, cleanse me of all evil, whatsoever evil it might be,
and fill me with your Spirit of love,
and help me to rest in and to live and work for this wonderful Spirit.

489.   ALL SINS AND SINFULNESS

Lord, I am sorry for all my sins, for all my wrongdoings in your sight;
Lord, I am sorry for all my sinfulness, for that which is repugnant to you in my mind, in my heart, in my soul and in my body.
Lord, I am sorry for all my sins and for my sinfulness;
Lord, have mercy; Christ have mercy; Lord, have mercy!

490.   LORD, I AM SORRY (3)

Lord, I am sorry; I am sorry; I am sorry.
Treat each person as God treats them, as a valued, precious person, that is, with the heavenly love.

491.   GOD'S MERCY (1)

Lord, I praise and thank you for doing your best.

492.   GOD'S MERCY (2)

Lord, I praise and thank you for the gift of life, and for the gift of death. Thank you, Lord, thank you.

Rose

493.   A WAY FORWARD (1)
Lord, I thank and praise you that you are always with me, that you are always constructive towards me; that you love me. Thank you, Lord! Praise be!

494.   A WAY FORWARD (2)
Lord, I thank and praise you that you call upon me to love you, your children, including myself, and your world. Thank you, Lord! Praise be!

495.   CHRISTMAS CELEBRATIONS
Lord, I thank and praise you for Christmas celebrations:
for carol concerts and services and street carol singing;
for parties and meals and friendly get togethers;
for visits to and stays with family and friends.
Lord, I thank and praise you for Christmas celebrations.
Thank you, Lord!

496.   IN YOUR WAY
Lord, help me to keep in your way of light, life and love, however your children may behave now and in the future. Praise be!

497.   LORD, HELP ME (1)
Lord, help me to love my neighbour in the way, or ways, that you would have me love my neighbour. Tenderly, delicately, vulnerably? Illuminatingly, critically, sufferingly? Lord, I submit myself to you and your way and ways. Have mercy upon me, Lord, have mercy.

498.   O LORD, FILL ME
O Lord, fill me with your love, that I might love in the way and ways that

you would have me love. O Lord, fill me!

499. FOR WHOLENESS

Lord, grant me your love and the wholeness which your love promotes, not only within myself, but between myself and others. Lord, grant me your love.

500. ONLY LOVE

Lord, you only love us, only act for our good. Help me to conduct myself in like manner, and so follow in your way, the way of love.

501. APPROPRIATELY

Lord, help me to pursue the goods of your kingdom, the goods of your Spirit, in all matters appropriately. Alleluia! Thank you, Lord.

502. INSTRUMENTS

Lord, help us to incarnate and to be instruments of your most holy Spirit in relation to all people, just as you are in relation to all people. Praise be!! Alleluia! Alleluia!

503. THIS DAY

Lord, I hold up to you this day and pray that your will will be done in it, as it is in heaven, as it is out of your great over-arching love. Praise be!

504. THANK YOU, LORD

Thank you, Lord, for being;
thank you, Lord, for being you;
thank you, Lord, for being what you are:
gracious, loving, merciful,
yes, Lord, merciful!

Thank you, Lord, thank you.

505. GOD'S ESSENTIAL GOODNESS
Lord, may I come to know and to appreciate and to love your essential goodness,
that goodness which knows no limits...
whether in terms of the multifaceted nature of life,
or in terms of the great variety of your children,
or indeed in terms of the extent of your world and word.
Lord, may I come to know and to appreciate and to love your essential goodness.
Alleluia!

506. LORD, HAVE MERCY (2)
Lord, have mercy, Lord, have mercy,
cleanse me of all that is offensive in your sight,
Lord, have mercy, Lord, have mercy.

Repeat as determined...

507. LORD, HELP ME (2)
Lord, help me, Lord, help me
to be the person that you would have me be,
to live the life that you would have me live;
to think the thoughts that you would have me think,
to say the words that you would have me say,
to do the deeds that you would have me do;
to conduct myself as you would have me conduct myself,
and to pursue those activities that you would have me pursue,
that in all things I may please you and praise your holy name,
in the name of Jesus our example, I ask it.

508.   ALL GOD'S CHILDREN
Lord, help me to love your children as you love them.

509.   IN ALL THINGS
Lord, help me to see the way forward at all times as loving my neighbour in all things. Thank you, Lord, thank you.

510.   THE WAY FORWARD
Lord, you are the way forward!
You are with me at all times,
You are constructive towards me at all times,
You love me! You are my only hope!

Lord, you are the way forward!
You are with my enemies at all times,
You are constructive towards my enemies at all times,
You love my enemies! You are their only hope!

Lord, you are the way forward!
You are with my enemies through me at all times,
You are constructive towards my enemies through me at all times,
You love my enemies through me! We are their only hope!

Lord, you are the way forward!
You are with us at all times,
You are constructive towards us at all times,
You love us! You are our only hope! Praise be!

511.   AN ESSENCE! (1)
Lord, I thank and praise you for revealing to me my self as an essence, as an essence which is to be valued, a distillate which is precious and unique!
Praise be!

512. AN ESSENCE! (2)
Lord, I thank and praise you for showing me my self as an essence, as a distilled essence! Praise be! Thank you, Lord!

513. THE ESSENCE
Lord, thank you for showing me the concept of essence, which in turn has led me to consider the essence of yourself, what it is, and what is its nature. Thank you, Lord!

514. AS ESSENCE
Lord, I thank and praise you for showing yourself as ESSENCE, the essence of the world in which we live, both animate and inanimate. Praise be! Thank you, Lord, thank you.

515. AN ESSENCE (3)
Lord, I thank and praise you for showing me my non-substantial self as an essence, and for helping me to realise that we all have such selves, selves which should be loved and respected, should be seen to be valuable and valued. Lord, I thank and praise you for this! Alleluia!

516. A SPIRIT WHICH IS LOVE
Lord, I adore you as a Spirit which is loving, from experiences of which we learn that you have the quality of love, and indeed might be said to be love.
Lord, I adore you as a Spirit which is loving!
Lord, I adore you as a Spirit which is love!

517. A SPIRIT WHICH IS PURE
Lord, you are a pure Spirit through and through.
Lord, you are intangible, powerful, ubiquitous and truly, totally pure.

Lord, you are a pure Spirit through and through forever more. Praise be!

518. A SPIRIT WHICH IS TRUTH
Lord, I adore you as a Spirit in whom every kind of truth coheres, and by whom all that is factually so is known. In you there is no supposition, fancy, illusion, false notion or imagining, for you are just the richness of truth, the fact of the matter in every sphere. Lord, I adore you as a Spirit who is truth, the whole truth and nothing but the truth. Praise be!

519. A SPIRIT WHICH IS BEAUTY
Lord, I adore you for the beauty of your Spirit;
I adore you for the beauty of your Spirit, I adore you for the beauty of your Spirit. Yes, Lord!
And I adore you for the beauty of the world around us,
which is the clothing of your Spirit,
and I adore you for the beauty which you reveal within us,
which is the expression of your Spirit.
Yes, Lord, I adore you for the beauty of your Spirit. Praise be!

520. A SPIRIT WHICH IS PRESENCE
Lord, I adore you for your presence, I adore you for your presence;
Lord, I adore you for your presence in our world, in our surroundings;
Lord, I adore you for your presence in ourselves or in another;
Lord, I adore you for your presence, I adore you for your presence.

521. PERTINENT WORDS
Lord, I adore you, I adore you, I adore you.
I adore you for your words, as when you inspire ideas,
and especially do I adore you for their relevance, their pertinence, to our goals and aspirations, to our hopes and fears, and to your purposes of love through us.

Lord, I adore you, I adore you, I adore you.

522. GOD'S INTELLIGENCE AND FORESEEING
Lord, I adore you,
I adore you for your intelligence in the physical universe,
the evolutionary physical universe.
Lord, I adore you.
I adore you for your intelligence in the animate world,
the evolutionary animate world.
Lord, I adore you.
I adore you for your intelligence in man's interior life,
man's evolutionary interior life.
Lord, I adore you.
Lord, I adore you. Lovely Lord!

523. LORD, I AM SORRY
Lord, I am sorry; I am sorry; I am sorry.
Here itmise particular matters about which you wish to be sorry…
Lord, I am sorry; I am sorry; I am sorry.

Treat each person as God treats them, as a valued, precious person, that is, with the heavenly love.

524. AS YOU LOVE
Lord, I am sorry that I have not loved your children, including myself, as you love them. Help me to love your children, including myself, as you love them this day and forever more.

The point and purpose of life is love, is agape. Therefore sin is that which is against love, against agape.
Sin is against God, and God is love.

525.   ALL WRONGDOINGS

Lord, I am sorry for all my wrongdoings in your eyes, and I am sorry for all the wrongdoings of others in your eyes. Thankyou for your forgiveness and healing.

During March 2001 I was penitent for certain sinful situations as our wrongdoing rather than my wrongdoing or theirs. I discovered that this was a clearly cleansing and healing thing to do.

526.   HOLY WEEK PRAYER (1)

Lord, let me not cast stones at sinners, but rather, as the donkey took Jesus to the citizens of Jerusalem, bring to them the spiritual nourishment which the Spirit has brought to me.

References: John 7v53 - 8v11 and John 12.

527.   HOLY WEEK PRAYER (2)

Lord, let me be sown in the soil of the Spirit, and may I die therein to be fruitful. May I grow trustingly out of the soil's darkness into the light and warmth of the Spirit and bear the harvest they engender. Praise be, O Lord.

528.   HOLY WEEK PRAYER (3)

Lord, let me not value the apprehensions of your children above your own.. May your view alone be my guide in my conduct and in my work. Yes, Lord!

529.   HOLY WEEK PRAYER (4)

Lord, my job is to feed your lambs. Let the food I provide be the daily bread with which you have nourished me during the years of my pilgrimage. May the bread of your light, your inspirations and insights, and your cleansings, provide the food I have for your lambs. Let me share it faithfully.

530. IN PARTICULAR (1)
Lord, I am sorry for my sins, in particular ....

Revelations of Divine Love, chapter 52, says: 'Quite rightly does our Lord will that we should accuse ourselves, and recognise, deliberately and honestly, our fall and the harm that follows. And since.....'

531. IN PARTICULAR (2)
Lord, I am sorry for my sins, in particular.......... And recognising that I can never make good the harm that has ensued, and will ensue, I throw myself upon your eternal love, mercy and forgiveness. Please help me to exercise restorative justice as far as this is humanly possible.
In chapter 53 of Revelations of Divine Love, Dame Julian tells us that we are always loved by God.

532. LOVE ALWAYS
Lord, show me where I have thought, spoken or acted against Holy Spirit love, and others also where I am involved, so that I may be contrite and penitent before you for these sins.

533. IN PARTICULAR (3)
Lord, I am sorry for my sins in particular knowing better than you.
Lord, help me to recognise your words and fall in line behind them.

534. WORSE THAN FOOT AND MOUTH
Lord, I have contracted the disease of evil; I am sorry, have mercy upon me; I am sorry, help me to get better.
Lord, disinfect the farm of my soul with your pure Spirit; sterilise every virus of evil from its pens, and cleanse its pastures for the sheep of your love.

535.   WANTON

Lord, I am sorry for all in my life that is wrong in your eyes. In particular disinfect me of all wantonness, and keep me in your way and show me how I may proceed in it.

536.   GOD IS TO BE LOVED

Lord, I am sorry where I have thought, spoken or acted in ways which are contrary to love of you, which do not harmonise with loving you, which do not express love for you. Please help me to love you, O living God, please help me to be Ray-love in relation to you this day and forever more.

537.   TO BE

O Lord, please help me to be the person that you would have me be, for, as Master Eckhart suggests, it is what I am that matters, rather than what I do. Being the person that you would have me be hopefully will mean that the things I do are the things that you would have me do. Praise be!

538.   FOR NOT AGAINST

O Lord, as Mother Julian suggests, all that I am and do is either for you or against you. Help me to be a person who is for you and whose conduct and activities flow from this being.

539.   HEAVENLY MOTHER (1)

Heavenly Mother, I beseech you for mercy and pity; heavenly Mother, I beseech you for help and grace.

540.   HEAVENLY MOTHER (2)

Heavenly Mother, I thank you for the fact that you made me; praise you for the fact that you uphold me by your grace; and beseech you that I may express your grace in and through my work, today and every day.

For Heavenly Mother (1) and (2) see R.D.L. chapter 54.

541.   HEAVENLY MOTHER (3)
Heavenly Mother, I pray that you will show me my wrongdoings, and how I may handle those wrongdoings appropriately in your eyes. I am sorry I have committed them and ask that you will forgive me for them.

542.   HEAVENLY MOTHER (4)
Heavenly Mother, when I love my neighbour it is my love I offer; I pray that in doing so I may also offer your love, that my love is instrumental in bringing your love to my neighbour this day and forever more.

543.   RATIONALITY
Lord, I thank and praise you for rationality, and for the empowerment which its proper and responsible use enables. And, Lord, I thank and praise you for love, which gives our rationality its proper purpose, and for man-woman relations which it similarly serves. Lord, I thank and praise you for rationality. Praise be to you!

544.   GOOD THINGS
Almighty God, I thank and praise you for good things: for good relationships, both same gender and opposite; and for good ideas, which can help us to be helpful. Let your Spirit, your love, your agape, inform all and be the measure of all. Wonderful Spirit! I thank and praise you for your good things!

545.   TOMORROW AND TOMORROW AND TOMORROW
Lord, I thank and praise you for love of, compassion for and solidarity

with everyone today, tomorrow and tomorrow and tomorrow. Thank you, Lord!

546. AIDS TO THE GODLY LIFE

Lord, I praise and thank you for the principles and attitudes which aid us in trying to live in tune with the Holy Spirit, for example, between partners, human love, human respect, human understanding and human communication. Thank you, Lord!

547. NOCTURNAL SUNSHINE

Lord God, I praise and thank you for your Spirit,
which is love, which is sunshine, which is healing;
I praise and thank you that I embody your Spirit,
and that in living-out that which I embody I have a life
which is love, which is sunshine, which is healing;
and I praise and thank you that it is in relation to your children and your world
that I live-out the life which you make possible for me:
which is love, which is sunshine, which is healing.

548. A HEAVENLY LOVER

Lord God, I praise and thank you that in your Spirit I have a lover, who is with me and within me both day and night, and however it may seem otherwise will not desert or betray me. Praise be!

549. APPROPRIATE KEY

Lord God, I praise and thank you that by the appropriate key we can release life in another, life which is love, which is sunshine, which is healing. Praise be and thank you!

550. INTEGRITY

Lord, I thank and praise you for integrity and in particular integrity in relation to my work for you, its objectives and its doing. May I show integrity in my re-actions to you and your world and in my expression of those re-actions in word and image. May I think and research as required with care, and articulate and express myself clearly and competently. Praise be!

551. THANKSGIVING FOR WORSHIP AND PRAYER

Lord, I thank and praise you for worship and prayer, both public and private; and I thank and praise you that we can speak to you at anytime. I recognise the inestimable privilege of worship and prayer, and thank and praise you that we are enabled to grow closer to you in and through them. Thankyou, Lord; praise be!

552. GOOD CHOICES

Lord God, help me to give sensible consideration to the pertinent factors before making a choice, before coming to a decision. Please, Lord. Praise be!

553. GOD'S INSPIRATIONS

Lord God, we recognise that we are strange mixes of good and bad. Notwithstanding there are times when you enlighten us and we go forward with renewed confidence and vigour, while at other times in our darkened minds we do not know which way to turn. Help us in the bad times to keep going in your ways and works, and in the good to try to retain the inspirations by which you help us to SEE! Praise be, Lord God!

554. TO OBTAIN PAID WORK

Lord, I pray that ——————— will obtain paid work, in particular I pray that ——————— will obtain the paid work of your choice. Thank you, Lord!

555. GRACIOUSNESS AND SURENESS
Lord, I pray that Holy Spirit graciousness and sureness will be my guide in the conduct of my life, Holy Spirit graciousness and sureness expressed in gracious and sure living, gracious and sure loving and gracious and sure illumining. Praise be!

556. FOR THE GOOD OF
Almighty God, I pray that you will assist me in aiming for the good of your self and of your children through acting and not acting appropriately. Help me to live-out this aim in all my relationships and various situations now, today and always.

557. A NEW YEAR PRAYER: FOR THE CONTINUATION OF GOD'S BLESSINGS
Almighty God, I ask that you will grant me a continuation of the blessings received during the year just ended. Pour down your blessings upon those for whom I pray and upon myself: thus may our lives be enriched, thus may they be made purposeful and enjoyable. As last year so this coming year and every year. Praise be to you, O Lord!

558. THANKS THAT I INCARNATE THE HOLY SPIRIT
Lord, I thank and praise you that I incarnate your most holy Spirit. I thank and praise you for this great privilege. Thank you, Lord!

559. THIS DAY
Lord God, I hold-up to you this day and ask for your continued blessing upon it. Help me to live this day in the love that you bestow this day. Praise be that I live in your love, whatever my choices, past or present. And I thank and praise you that you love all, value all, equally. Help me to remember this, and to rejoice in it both for others and for myself. You are love and love all equally this day! THIS DAY!

560. HUMAN (1)
Lord, help me to bring human love to all and all situations this day.

561. HUMAN (2)
Lord, I thank and praise you that I am a human being. Help me this day and every day to be a good human being.

In 'Revelations of Divine Love' Mother Julian says in chapter 51 that 'the white coat is his flesh; its being single the fact that there is nothing separating GODHEAD and human nature'.

562. HUMAN (3)
Lord, help me to be a human human being this day, and even from time to time a good one, to wit, a human being who shows forth a little of your Godhead. Yes, Lord! Praise be!

563. THE GIFT OF CHOICE (1)
Lord God, I thank you for the gift of choice and for the empowerment it affords, for example, the opportunity to shape the present moment, both practically and morally. Lord, I thank you for the gift of choice and pray that you will help me to use this gift better with each succeeding day. Praise be!

564. FOR THE GOOD OF ALL
Lord, help me to act for the good of all, including ....NAME(S).........., and especially in the ways you have deputed to me, are deputing and will depute, today and tomorrow and tomorrow and tomorrow till I depart this life. Thank you, Lord! Praise be!

565. REGARDING CONDUCT FOR CLOSE PERSONS

Father, I pray that ———— and myself will conduct our relationship in ways which are pleasing to you, and that we shall avoid conducting ourselves in ways which are displeasing to you. I am sorry for any conduct of ours which has given you offence and I ask for your forgiveness. Grant us also your inspiration to assist us in a fresh start.

566. REGARDING THE WAY FORWARD FOR CLOSE PERSONS

Lord God, show the way forward for ———— and myself, today, tomorrow and always. I pray that the future will unfold in ways which are pleasing to you, and that we shall set our faces against ways which are displeasing to you. Lord God, show the way forward for ———— and myself. Yes, Lord!

567. A VOCATIONAL PRAYER

Lord, let me go in peace with you
to love and to serve you,
this day and this night and always.
Thank you, Lord.

568. THE WAY FORWARD (1)

Lord, I thank and praise you for thinking and feeling and choosing, and that this is the modus operandi for living our lives, and for going forward in the way of the Holy Spirit and of Holy Spirit love.

569. THE WAY FORWARD (2)

Lord, help me to prosecute this day my imperfect human love, subjecting it all the while to the searchlight of your Holy Spirit love, its purposes and its judgement.

570. FOR THE FIRST OF THE MONTH
(and afterwards as required)

Lord, I pray that during the coming month you will show me what in your eyes is wrong in my life and how I may put it right or begin to put it right. Rightness before you is all I look for in this life and I earnestly beseech your support in my seeking for it. Yes, Lord, I earnestly beseech your support.

571. A SUBMISSION

Lord, I pray that I will think, speak and act harmoniously with your Spirit, with your will, and undertake the Spirit-work, the love-work, which you assign to me this coming day, in the future and for evermore.

572. LORD JESUS

Lord Jesus, I love you;
Lord Jesus, I love you;
Lord Jesus, I love you.

573. LORD, HELP ME!

LORD, HELP ME to love; Lord, help me to say in effect 'I love you'.

LORD, HELP ME to obey your commands, and in particular the commandment 'to love one another'.

LORD, HELP ME to conduct myself properly, help me to say in effect 'child of God'.

LORD, HELP ME to think 'what is best', and how best to achieve this, for any of your children in any interaction I may have with them. Lord, help me!

574. SELF OBLATION (1)

Lord, I give myself to you in my totality, body and mind and soul. Yes, Lord, I give myself to you.

575. SELF OBLATION (2)

Lord, keep me by the power of your Holy Spirit from any thinking, saying or doing which is contrary to your will, anything which is evil, today and everyday.

576. REGARDING A PROBLEM

Lord, have mercy upon me with regard to my problems and in particular *[...state the particular problem...]*.

Clarify to me the nature of my problem, and help me to accept that I do indeed have it.

Inspire me with ideas as to how I might deal with this problem, *[...state the particular problem...]*, with a view to bringing about an improvement in our situation and in our relationship(s), even maybe a resolution of it. And help me to implement your inspirations sensibly and sensitively, and indeed all the pertinent and helpful ideas I have available to me. Thankyou, Lord.

577. JUSTLY

JUSTLY (1)

Lord, open the eyes of my mind with respect to justice.

JUSTLY (2)

Lord, I pray that I may behave fairly and justly to all, to everyone, those who have my well-being at heart and those who do not.

JUSTLY (3)

Lord, I pray that you will uphold in me a sense of justice, of treating people fairly, and in legal matters with justice.

578. PRAYERS FOR CONCLUDING INTERCESSIONS

Indeed I hold-up to you, Lord, all those for whom I pray and ask that you will pour down your light, life and love upon each and everyone of us, that each of us

(select one of the following)
1. might try to be instruments of your light, life and love, instruments of your most holy Spirit, in relation to everyone

2. might try to be more the person that you would have us be,
live more the life that you would have us live,
and do more the things that you would have us do

3. might be an instrument of your father and mother love, of your Spirit love

4. might be good in our being and in our doing and in our not doing

5. might be lamps of light, life and love, and shine brightly for all and enliven and warm all
(concluding)
this day and forever more.

579.   OUR GARDENS
Lord God, we thank and praise you that we each and every one have gardens which we can love and tend, gardens which contain our work and interests, our homes and families, and our religion. Lord God, we thank and praise you for these. May our lives include those relationships and pursuits that you would have us have as apects of our lives. May all the relationships we have, and all the things we do, be pursued with love and interest and devotion, for the betterment of our lives in the present and in time to come. Praise be to you, O Lord God.

580.   PRISMS OF LOVE
Lord, we thank and praise you for the prisms which you have put in place and developed through evolution for the good of your children, whether physical or biological, social or religious, and pray that we shall have our eyes opened to the loves which they variously defract, and seeing these loves try to deploy and enhance them, to capitalise on them,

for the good of one another and to your glory.
We thank and praise you for your prisms of love!

581. THE WAYS WHICH ARE GOOD

Lord God, help us to live our lives in the ways which are good in your eyes. Illumine our minds, strengthen our inner beings and bring us always to see the ways of love in whatever relationship or situation or activity we are presently engaged in. Let the imperfections in our lives be dealt with also in the ways which are good in your eyes. May the spiritual sword of truth be ever ready to defend us and to promote the wonderful truth of yourself and the ways which are good in your eyes. Lord God, we thank and praise you for your light.

582. THE GIFT OF CHOICE (2)

Holy God, we praise and thank you for the gift of choice.
Help us to try to use this wonderful gift sensibly, to try to make good choices in all of life's varied departments, such as our conduct, our relationships and our work.
Holy God, we praise and thank you for the gift of choice.
Especially do we ask you that you will speak clearly in any particular matter in which you seek to guide us, so that in the exercise of our reason and our judgement we may be enabled to make appropriate and wise choices in giving effect to your guidance.
Holy God, we praise and thank you for the gift of choice.
By it we can choose to do many wonderful things, follow you, worship you, work for you and love our neighbour. Uphold those choices which are pleasing in your eyes and oppose those which are displeasing. Thus may we aspire to be the people that you would have us be and live the lives that you would have us live.
Holy God, we praise and thank you for the gift of choice.

583. HIDDEN ABUNDANCE

Lord, in the nothingness within and around us let us discover the

richness of your Being and the delights of your Creation.
Lord, out of the nothingness within and around us let us create those good things which accord with your Being and hint at your Creation.
Lord, from the nothingness within and around us let us share the illuminations and love of your Being and our experience of your Creation.
Lord, from our nothingness let there be shown forth your abundance this day and forever more.

584. THE PROBLEM OF EVIL
Heavenly Father, I hold-up to you the problem of evil. How did it come into being, in what does it consist? Please illumine my mind in respect to these matters. Recently I asked someone sitting next to me for his definition of evil and he said that he thought it was extreme hatred. Certainly extreme hatred would be the antithesis of the two great commandments and so is a helpful contribution in this matter.
I thank you for the light I have received upto now with respect to this problem: thank you.

585. AS YOU ARE, SO LET US BE!
Servant God, help us to get to know you, to know what is your nature and your character. In knowing your character may we aspire to model ourselves upon you, to regard you as a perfect example, and attempt to conduct ourselves appropriately, for the ways which are right for you are also right for us. Help us to care as you care, in our everyday conduct and in our daily work, so that the world is a better place, today, tomorrow and in the years to come. As you are, so let us be!

586. 'THAT WE MAY PERFECTLY LOVE YOU'
Heavenly King, we pray that you will help us in this tremendous aspiration to perfectly love you.
Heavenly King! May our worship of you express our love of you in adoration, praise, thanksgiving, confession and supplication, and may our

conduct and activities in our day to day living be worthy of a holy Spirit of love.

Heavenly King! May the things we do honour you and your world! Help us to perfectly love you as you are!

587.   ONLY-LOVE

Lord, I offer my love to my neighbour. May it be all that I have to offer. May it also be an expression of your love: may my love be the covers for the wonderful book which is your love for your children. I pray that I may seek to express consciously and conscientously that of you within myself, your perfect love for each and everyone, for we are each and everyone the apple of your eye! Yes, Lord!

588.   PRAYERS FOR REPETITION

Lord, I adore you...
Father, I adore you...
As Father, I adore you...
Help me to front you, Father...
Help me to enact you, Father...
Help me to express you, Lord...
Help me to be your word, Lord...

589.   FOR LEADINGS AND OPPOSINGS

Lord, I adore and praise you that you communicate with your children and that you communicate as you do. I adore and praise you for the pertinence of your communications, relevant to the manner in which we live our lives and to our present activities and actions. Lord, I adore and praise you that you communicate with your children and that you communicate as you do.

590.   FOR THE PRIMACY OF LOVE

Lord, I adore and praise you for the primacy of love:
for the primacy of love between people,

for the primacy of love between you and your children,
for you are love, for you are agape,
spirit love in your spirit nature and spirit character.
Lord, I adore and praise you for the primacy of love!

591.   ADORATION
ADORATION (1)
Lord, I adore you as a merciful God;
Lord, I adore you as a forgiving God;
Lord, I adore you as a God in whom my joy is complete.
Praise be!

ADORATION (2)
Lord, I adore you in and for yourself:
Lord, I adore you; Lord, I adore you;
Lord, I adore you.   Repeat as appropriate.

ADORATION (3)
Heavenly Father, I adore you.
Heavenly Father, I adore you.
Heavenly Father, I adore you.
Repeat with: Lord Jesus Christ; Most Holy Spirit.

592.   INNER SPRING
Lord, I adore you as an INNER SPRING, which welling-up unendingly,
PROMOTES ETERNAL LIFE. Praise be!
Lord, I adore you for this WONDERFUL GIFT. May I appreciate it and utilise it POSITIVELY, thus promoting eternal life on your behalf. Praise be!

593.   THE ADORATION OF AGAPE
O Agape, I adore you... (repetition as required)

and pray that you will help me to express you, O Agape, in my daily life.

594. ADORATION OF THE SPIRIT
Lord, I adore You as profound Spirit;
Lord, I adore You as profound Spirit, the chief quality of which is love;
Lord, I adore You as profound Spirit, as the One who benefits all and who can only benefit all, as the One from whom the heavenly manna comes. Praise be!

595. CONTRITION (1)
Lord, I am sorry for my sins whatever they may be; help me to live-out your Christ Spirit, your Love Spirit, today and always.

596. CONTRITION (2)
Lord, I am sorry for my sins whatever they may be in your eyes; help me to live-out your Spirit, your Motherhood, in love and kindness, wisdom, knowledge and goodness, today and always.

The qualities of motherhood courtesy Mother Julian, R.D.L. 60.

597. CONTRITION (3)
Lord, I am sorry for my sins. (3x)
Lord, I am sorry for our sins. (3x)
Help us, notwithstanding our sins, to be rocks of your caring love, today and for evermore.

598. IN YOUR EYES
Lord, I am sorry for all my wrongdoings in your eyes and for my imperfect nature. Protect me from all those things which, in your eyes, are unnatural or unproductive, and uphold me in all those things which are good and wholesome.

St. Giles, Hartington

In your eyes, Lord, for never am I out of their sight. Praise be!

599. NOT TRANSFORMATION, BUT CHOICE

Awaiting the possibility of transformation, Lord, I pray that while I am here on earth I will choose to utilise all the constituents of life to serve your purposes of love for your creation in soul-engaging, soul-enduing ways this day and forever more.

600. THE SPIRIT (1)

Lord, I thank and praise you for your Spirit and its manifestations:
for its manifestations in inspiration and insight, in loving suggestion and guidance, and in life and new life.
I thank and praise you for your Spirit and its manifestations:
for its manifestations received within me, and for those received from others and your world outside of me, today, tomorrow and every day.

601. BROTHER DEATH

Father, we thank and praise you for Brother Death, for, in the light of his sure ministration, we can seek to define our important principles and purposes, our priorities and preferences, and seek to live in the light of them until he ministers to us. Praise be.

602. FOR INSPIRATIONS AND INSIGHTS

Lord, I thank and praise you for insights and inspirations,
for guidance and useful information,
regarding the living of our lives,
our conduct and our activities.
Lord, I thank and praise you for these,
especially as they form expressions
of your love for your children. Praise be!

603. THANKS FOR WORSHIP

Lord, I thank and praise you for private worship, in particular the opportunity to be sorry and to offer you myself and my love and deep respect.

I thank and praise you that I, a single human being, a product of the great, slow-turning wheels of evolution, can engage with the Mover of those same great, slow-turning wheels. Lord, I thank and praise you for private worship. Praise be!

604. FOR GOD'S ADDRESS

Lord, I thank and praise you for your address, directly through your most Holy Spirit and indirectly through your children and your world.

And I thank and praise you for the opportunities we have to respond to that address in our worship and in our work, whether through art or action.

Lord, I thank and praise you for your address!

605. GOD'S PRESENCE

Lord, I thank and praise you for your constant presence. Thankyou for accompanying me on the road of life and thankyou for your generous inputs as we travel along. Help me to remember that they are expressions of your love for me, that they are for my benefit. Thankyou!

606. THAT I MAY LOVE MYSELF

Lord, I pray that I may love myself, and that you will teach me how I may do so. Assist me in acting for my good in relation to the different aspects of my being. So may I be the person that you would have me be, whole and rounded and fully grown. Thank you, Lord.

607. LIVING BEFORE AND FOR GOD

Lord God, help me to live before and for You, as You would have me live before and for You.

608. LOVING BEFORE AND FOR GOD
Lord God, help me to think love, speak love and do love, and so serve you, the Spirit of Love.

609. TO HEAR GOD
Lord, I pray that you will help me today to accept you as you are;
to accept that you communicate as you do,
and to accept all your communications of whatever kind, recognising that they are expressions of your love. Lovely Lord!

610. THE LORD'S GOOD THINGS
Lord, I thank and praise you for your good things.
Fill my mind with these things,
and help me in my trying to fill my life with them
this day and everyday.
Lord, I thank and praise you for your good things.

611. REGARDING VISION
Lord, grant me the vision that you would have me have regarding my conduct in relation to you and your children, and the work that you would have me do for you and your children and the manner in which I do it, that at all times and in all matters I may manifest your Spirit.
Lord, may I make visible the invisible, your most Holy Spirit. Yes!

612. INSPIRATIONS
Lord, teach me how to conduct myself as you would have me conduct myself, in particular how you would have me respond to 'inspirations', to verbal Spirit surges.

613.　THE SPIRIT (2)
Lord, help me to live out your Spirit, your Spirit of love, of light, of life, in relation to all people, whatever their occupation, whatever their outlook, this day and every day.

614.　MORNING PRAYER
Lord, I pray that we may be respect and love and peace in relation to You, each other, ourselves and your world during the coming day.

615.　FOR THE INNER SPRING
Lord, do not take your Holy Spirit from me, but let it remain in and around me and well-up, throughout my life, to promote those things which are good in your eyes. Praise be!

616.　FOR BLESSING
Lord, pour down your blessing on those for whom I pray, your light that we might know you better, your life that we might live more abundantly and your love that we might love more generously, today and everyday.

617.　LORD, OPEN MY EYES!
I have sometimes thought, Lord, that penitence ranks highest amongst the different sorts of prayer employed by your children. Is there a more precious sight in your eyes than tears of penitence? They are the very antithesis of that hardness of heart, that self-righteousness, which Jesus found so objectionable.
Lord, open my eyes! Let me see with your eyes! And seeing with your eyes the true nature of my conduct, if I find anything wrong in it, any pertinent good omitted, let me confess my wrongdoing, or my omission, and be deeply contrite for it.
I thank you for the opportunities you give us to say sorry for the wrongdoings we have done and for the good-doings we have not. I

thank you for the precious gift of penitence.
Lord, open my eyes! Let me see with your eyes!

618. FOR THE DIVINE LOVE
Lord, I thank and praise you for your love for your children, and pray that I will sink into it as I might sink into an armchair. May I be content to act only in so far as your love supports and finds expression in what I say and do. Grant me a clear mind and a sensitive inner being, out of which your love might rise up and be shared in your world. Praise be!

619. GOOD OUT OF EVIL
Lord, it is sadly true that evil is necessarily a part of our lives, both in ourselves and in others. Let us have a positive attitude towards this state of affairs and seek to make the best use of all experience, the dark as well as the light. Help us to try to nurture good from evil, as if we were trying to bring on seedlings in a desert, giving good things our tender, patient care. Thus may your kingdom come, your good be realised on earth, today and every day.

620. TO LOVE GOD
Lord, you will that I love you; let me know, please, how I might love you, today, tomorrow and always.

621. LORD, I LOVE AND ADORE YOU
Lord, I love and adore you both for yourself, and for the things you look for between your children.
Lord, I love and adore you for being the One who truly is; (v.28)
Lord, I love and adore you for being the One from whom streams of living water flow; (v.38)
Lord, I love and adore you for being the One who looks to our being just in our judgements of one another; (v.24)
And, Lord, I love and adore you for being the One who looks to our

having a care for one another.
Lord, I love and adore you.

The verse references are from St. John, chapter 7.

622. PASS THE PARCEL
Lord, I love and adore you...
Lord, I love and adore you as the One who places his children in the position of playing 'pass the parcel', and asks that we pass on to our neighbour a parcel which contains your good things, rather than our hurts and humiliations, which parcel we must not pass on.
Lord I love and adore you...

623. LIGHT! LOVE! LIFE!
Lord, I love and adore you for your Self;
Lord, I love and adore you for your gifts:
for the illumination you bring to my mind,
for the love you bring to my heart,
and for the life you bring to my body;
Lord, I love and adore you for your Self and for
your wonderful gifts. Praise be!

624. WASH THE FEET
Lord, I adore you and love you, for you are light, life and love!
Lord, I thank and praise you that I am a vessel of your Spirit, of your light, life and love!
Lord, I ask you to help me to think, feel and choose:
light, as I see and understand it, rather than darkness and disquiet;
life, as I see and understand it, rather than death and denial;
love, as I see and understand it, rather than hatred and rejection.
Lord, I thank and praise you that I may wash your children's feet with good things, hopefully to a degree your good things.
Lord, I adore you and love you, for you are light, life and love! Praise be!

625. A GOD TO LOVE
Lord, I adore you as a pure and holy God;
Lord, I adore you as a God to love;
Lord, I adore you as a pure and holy God.

626. A GOD TO LOVE (2)
Lord, I adore you as a God to love;
Lord, I adore you as a God whom I have no choice but to love!
Lord, I adore you with love and respect, with great regard and tenderness.

627. AS A HOLY GOD
Lord, I adore you as a holy God,
in all, yet separate,
as a holy God,
profound power,
as a holy God,
perfectly pure,
as a holy God,
unpredictable, yet always pertinent.
Lord, I adore you as a holy God,
as a holy God.

628. UNIVERSALLY PRECIOUS
Almighty God, help me to be and to express your Holy Spirit in relation to all people, irrespective of their physical appearance and any particular merits and demerits they may have in this regard.
All people have their strengths and weaknesses, their especial gifts and abilities, their particular attractiveness, and in any case all are uniquely precious in your eyes.
Lord, help me to be and to express your Holy Spirit, your Light, in relation to all.

629. IN YOUR SIGHT
Lord, I hold-up to you myself and confess all the things I think, say and do which are wrong in your sight; all the things in my being which are wrong in your sight; and I am deeply sorry for them all. Lord God, have mercy upon me and forgive me for all those things. Have mercy upon me; have mercy upon me.

630. AGAINST YOU AND THAT OF YOU
Lord, I am sorry for everything that I have thought, said and done, and have been in my being, which was against you, against your character or your nature. And I am sorry for everything that I have thought, said and done, and have been in my being, which was against that of you in your children, against your character or your nature in them.
Lord, I am sorry, I am contrite; have mercy upon me, have mercy upon me.

631. PRAYER OF PENITENCE
Lord, most holy Spirit,
I am sorry for my sins and my sinfulness,
for my wrongdoing and my wrongbeing in your sight,
and especially am I with regard to .... STATE
Lord, most holy Spirit,
help me, and especially with regard to .... STATE
to try to improve my game,
to try to do better in all of life's various aspects
Lord, help me; Lord, help me; Lord, help me.

632. WALL OF LOVE
Lord, I am sorry for my lack of humbleness, for my lack of submitting myself to You.
Help me to live-out the Wall of Love Presence, to become a wall of love. Praise be.

633.   ANY SUGGESTIONS?
Lord, if you have any suggestions as to how I might improve my conduct in relation to You, do please make them.

634.   THE FIRE WHICH BURNS
Lord, I thank and praise you for your pruning activities, for the fact that you cut away barren branches, and clean those which do fruit in order that they may fruit better.
Lord, I thank and praise you that you gather-up the withered branches, pile them up and make a fire of them, reducing them thus to ash. Fortunately this is not necessarily the end of the story. The ash can be used as fertiliser, which also can assist the fruitful branches to be yet more fruitful.
Lord, I thank and praise you for your pruning activities, and that the barren branches can have a place in your cycle of fruitfulness.

See John 15, verses 1-8.

635.   FOR THE GIFTS OF LIFE AND OF TIME
Lord, I thank and praise you for the gift of life, for the gift of being,
for being which is physical, for being which is mental,
for being which is emotional, for being which is spiritual.
Lord, I thank and praise you for the gift of life, for the gift of being. And also, Lord, I thank and praise you for the gift of time, and for the opportunities which it affords,
for the opportunity to live, for the opportunity to love,
and for the opportunity to point to You.
Lord, I thank and praise you for the gift of time, and for the opportunities which it affords. Praise be!

636.   SIGNS AND SIGNALS
Lord, I thank and praise you for the life of ——————- and the signs

and signals of transcendence which he/she displayed, pointers to you!
And I thank and praise you for purpose in life in general, and for the particular purpose you have given to each one of us. Praise be!

637. FOR PENITENCE
Almighty God, I thank and praise You for PENITENCE, for the opportunities You give your children to say sorry for their wrong-doings and their wrong being, and for the possibilities You afford of renewal and of starting again, and of attempting to travel in the ways You would have us go. Praise be!

638. LITTLE BITS!
Lord, be with me in my little bits of living, loving and illumining; lead, inspire and direct them to your purposes of love; so may your will be done, your work implemented. Praise be!

639. GOOD FRIDAY PRAYER
Lord, I ask that I may not crucify you in any way shape or form;
I ask that I may not crucify you by behaving in ways which are contrary to your character, for example, by thinking or speaking in crude or lewd language; I ask that I may not crucify you by hurting or harming any of your children.
Lord, I ask that I may not crucify you in any way whatsoever, today and in the future.

640. FOR YOUR SPIRIT
Lord, help me, as ash★, to provide nutrients for your Spirit;
     as a human being, to be glass for your Spirit;
and, as a worker, to be patient for your Spirit.

★See John 15, verses 1-8.

641. WORTH MY BEST
Lord, I thank and praise You that in Your eyes all Your children are of infinite worth, and that therefore all Your children are equally worth my best, my best conduct, my best love and loving, are equally worth my best thinking, speaking and practical action. Praise be!

642. A PRAYER FOR THE NIGHT WATCHES
The following prayer was created when I lay awake one night recently. As it was created during the night it could be that it is suitable for use during the night, although not only then, of course. Anyway, the title is okay.

Most Holy God, most Holy Spirit,
I give myself to you, head, heart and body,
lock, stock and barrel. By the power of your Spirit
cleanse me of all evil, fill me with your good Self,
redeem me from all sinfulness, heal me of all disease,
and protect me against all temptation,
this night and always. Praise be!

I also made a prayer with a play on my name, I think at the same time.

643. A PRAYER FOR THOSE WHOSE NAME IS ——★
Lord, may I be a ray of your Spirit sunshine,
and ask that you will uphold my shining of
——★ love, light and life,
——★ peace, patience and purity.
Make of my rays vehicles of
your Spirit love, light and life,
your Spirit peace, patience and purity,
this day and always. Praise be!

★ ANY NAME

644. AS A GOOD SPIRIT
Almighty God, I adore and praise you as a Good Spirit, as a Love Spirit, as an Agape Spirit; and I adore you and praise you that you are such a Being, have such a character.
In you I find my Treasure, my Hope, my Confidence, my Trust, my Always.
Heavenly Father, I adore and praise you, praise and adore you.

645. AS ONE WHO IS PURE
Lord, I love and adore you as one who is pure, unsullied, of one unblemished nature, flawless, wholesome through and through, unalloyed, of depthless purity.
Lord, I love and adore you as one who is pure. Praise be!

646. AS ONE WHO IS ALWAYS RIGHT
Lord, Holy Spirit, I love and adore you as the one who is always right, as the one in whom complete confidence may be reposed. Help me to be guided by you, whilst retaining my humanity, my need to see rationally that what I am doing is right, is appropriate.

647. GREAT SOURCE
Lord, I love and adore you as the source of LOVE*, through your Spirit, through your people, both earthly and heavenly, and through your wonderful creation. Lord, I love and adore you.
*Repeat with LIGHT and LIFE.

648. RAYS OF YOUR SHINE
Lord, I love and adore you:
for the daytime, when we may pursue our legitimate concerns;
for life appearing to be an unadulterated nightmare;

for the fact that we are your children, children of your Light, of your Shine;
and for the fact that we may be rays of your Shine, of your Light.
Lord, I love and adore you.

649.   AS YOU ARE (1)
Lord, I lovingly adore you as you are, whatever is your actual nature, however you have behaved and do behave towards me. Lord, I lovingly adore you as you are.

650.   AS YOU ARE (2)
Lord, I lovingly adore you as you have been, as you are and as you will be, always the same.

651.   TEACH ME
Lord, teach me to adore you as you would have me adore you. Lord, teach me.

652.   AS ONE WHO WASHES OUR FEET
Lord, I adore you as One who washes our feet by inspiring us with helpful ideas and gentle guidances with respect to the life we live for you, and by bathing us in the beauties of your world. Lord, I adore you as One who washes our feet.

653.   AS THE ONE WHO WASHES OUR FEET
Lord, I adore you as the one who washes our feet with grace: for example, the graces of illumination and guidance. Lord, let us also wash feet with grace, you grace: let us also be sources of illumination and guidance, this day and every day.

654. A SORRY PRAYER

Lord God, rightly or wrongly, I exist, I am alive. While I am on earth help me to love. This seems as good a way as any of utilising my time before my demise - and perhaps afterwards as well. Thankyou, Lord.

655. SETTLED

Lord, I am sorry I have not been settled in the fact of you, of me in you, and you in me, and of living out you in my life.

Lord, let me be settled in me being in you, and you being in me, and me living out you, your love and your creativity, in my life today and every day.

656. TEACH ME

Lord, teach me how I might become like you.
After R.D.L. 77, last four sentences.

657. HELP ME TO LOVE MYSELF

Lord, I am sorry for not loving, in particular for not loving myself. Help me to love myself today and every day.

658. LIVE LOVE

Lord, help to live love from moment to moment, to do whatever I do in fact with love. LOVE! LOVING!

659. I HAVE NOT

Lord God, I am sorry this week particularly with regard to those things which I should have said and done. Show me clearly those things about which you would have me speak and act and especially those things about which I have not spoken and acted in the past. Guide and strengthen me in the doing of the same this week, next and every week.

660.   TO PROMOTE, TO CHANGE
Lord God, strengthen us in speaking and acting to promote those things which uphold your love, and to change those things which contradict it. May we value and appreciate you, your work and works, and also your children, their work and works; and seek to change those things which should not be, such as injustice. Lord God, help us to make the world a better place.

661.   LORD, I AM SORRY (1)
Lord, I am sorry for my imperfections, for my wrongdoings in your sight, for my evil spirit. Lord, I am sorry.
Have mercy, have mercy upon me, have mercy.
Lord, aid and support me in NOT crucifying you today. Lord, aid and support me.
Have mercy, have mercy upon me, have mercy.

662.   LORD, I AM SORRY (2)
Lord, I am sorry for all my wrongdoings.
In your way, please forgive me for these.
Thankyou, Lord.

663.   LORD, I AM SORRY (3)
Lord, I am sorry for my wrongdoings in your sight, those which have arisen from neglect, as well as those which I have thought, said and done. Show me those wrongdoings in particular for which you would have me repent and be contrite. Lord, I submit myself to you and give you my full attention.
   PRAYER AS IT SUGGESTS ITSELF. CONCLUDING:
Lord, I am sorry; have mercy, have mercy.

664.   LOVE RESOURCES
Almighty God, I thank and praise you for illumination, either from

Heaven by inspiration, or from your children and their multifaceted media. And I thank and praise you for love resources, for Heaven, for your children, including myself, and for your world, all love resources, all sources of illumination, all repositories of the love of God!

665. WITHIN

Lord, holy God, I praise and thank you for the fact that your Kingdom is within me; help me not to sully it in any way shape or form with vile thoughts, words or deeds. If I should do so may I be sorry for my vileness and be forgiven for the same. Let no evil be within me. Praise and thanks be for your holy Name and Kingdom.

666. FOR LOVE

Lord God, I thank and praise you for ... (for example, a religious paper or magazine), for your inspirations, your words of love, and for having a purpose in life, which is to be and to do love, your love, this day and forever.

667. FOR PHYSICAL LIFE

Lord God, I thank and praise you for the physical beings with which you have endowed us, the products of aeons of development and evolution; and today I especially thank you for the many vital functions our bodies have, maintaining species continuity as well as individual, and recognising their extra-ordinary organisation. Lord God, I thank and praise you for these.

668. THE FRAGRANCE OF YOUR PRESENCE

Lord, I thank and praise you for the fragrance of your presence:
of your upholding, supportive presence;
of your guiding, restraining presence;
or your healing, redeeming presence.

Lord, I thank and praise you for the fragrance of your presence.

669. FOR CARING
Lord, I thank and praise You for your Spirit,
for occasionally occasioning hope;
for caring for others, for caring for myself;
for lightheartedness, play and rest;
and for the opportunity to be a beam of your Shine.
Lord, I thank and praise You for your Spirit.

670. THE GATEWAY
Lord God, I thank and praise you for love, friendliness and redemption, and that my home can be a place of love, friendliness and redemption, can be, indeed, A GATEWAY TO THE SPIRIT! I thank and praise you, Lord God!

671. A DYNAMIC RELATIONSHIP
Lord, I thank and praise you that you exist, and that your world is in a dynamic relationship with you, and in particular ourselves, your children.

672. A CENTRE
Lord, I thank and praise you that you provide a centre to our lives, a centre of interest, a focal area in the picture of our lives.

673. FOR DRAWING AND PAINTING
Lord, I thank and praise you on behalf of all who draw and paint:
for the lovely colours and different mediums available today;
for the beautiful books about artists, and different ways of approaching drawing and painting;
and for the opportunities to share with others, in clubs and societies, in exhibitions and individually.

Lord, I thank and praise you on behalf of all who draw and paint.

674. THE BRITISH POLICE SERVICE
Lord, speak your light, life and love in the lives of all the Chief Constables and officers who work in the British Police Service. Thank you, Lord.

675. THE RELIGIOUS SOCIETY OF FRIENDS
Lord, I hold up to you the members of the R.S.F., those who join in with them, and all who use their meeting houses, for whatever reason. Lord, we are all in your Spirit, and your Spirit is in all of us.

676. MY ENEMIES
Lord, I hold up to you my enemies, and, indeed, all those who misbehave towards their neighbours, for whatever reason and in whatever manner. Lord, we are all in your Spirit and your Spirit is in all of us.

677. A SYLLOGISM?
Lord, all are souls;
all souls are regarded by YOU with the eye of love;
THEREFORE, WE should regard all souls with the eye of love.

678. SUFFERING
Lord, help us to suffer, for example, the injustices of life, in respect to the legal system, to illness, to man's hatred of his fellows, to accidents. Show us what suffering entails, the pain, hurt, damage, destruction, and how we might deal with our suffering. It is right not to mind the little stings, but what about the big ones? Lord, help us to suffer.

679. PRAYER FOR CLEANSING
O Lord, cleanse me and heal me of all evil spirit, of all resentment, of

all coarse thoughts and thinkings. Please, Lord, I beg and beseech you.

680. LIVE OUT
Lord, help me to live out your most holy Spirit, a Spirit which is profound love, amazing intelligence and unending creativity. Lord, help me to live out your most holy Spirit.

681. TO REMAIN FAITHFUL
Lord, let me keep in your ways, your ways of agape, in respect to our spiritual and physical needs, for you are greater than any earthly power, far greater. Let me devote myself to your good things, your things of beauty, your things of love, and remain faithful in these things rather than desert to the enemy, to evil.

682. 24/7 (1)
Almighty God, I thank you for my calling, which is to point to you. Help me to pursue my calling, seriously and earnestly within a framework of twenty-four seven. Thank you, Lord.

683. IN YOUR SPIRIT
Lord, I thank and praise you that we live in your Spirit and that your Spirit lives in us. Praise be!

684. A THANKYOU
Lord God, I thank you for reflection and prayer, for the opportunity to think about personal matters and to share them with you; and I thank you for your responses to my communing, your inspirations and insights. Praise be!

685. THE POINT AND PURPOSE OF LIFE IS LOVE
Love! your love! the point and purpose of life is love!
Lord, I am contented in this proposition, and affirm that I shall attempt to live it out.
Love! your love! the point and purpose of life is love!

686. 24/7 (2)
Lord, help me to point to you rationally in all matters twenty-four seven.

687. TO POINT TO GOD
Lord, help me to point to you. To that end help me to behave towards others and myself as you behave towards me, and help me also not to crucify you in any way, shape or form.

688. SECRET AGENT
Lord, help me to be an agent of your love in relation to all: all people, including myself; all things.

689. GRACE GRACIOUSLY
Lord, I live in your grace and your grace lives in me. Help me to live your grace graciously.

690. NO DEMANDS BUT THE DEMANDS OF LOVE
Lord, help me to organise my day around the demands of love, so that my thought, words and deeds* are guided by and meet those demands. Lord, help me!
*deeds: acts, actions, activities.

691. THE WAY FORWARD
O Heavenly Word, I see the way forward as a continuum of LOVINGS

and of SUFFERINGS, where-in we seek our good and absorb our evil. Help me to live loving thoughts, words and deeds, and to suffer imperfect, even evil, thoughts, words and deeds, in others and in myself, today and every day. Praise be!

692. LOVE SPIRIT!

Lord, I incarnate you, LOVE SPIRIT.
Help me to live in all particulars as one who incarnates you, LOVE SPIRIT.
Help me to remember that others incarnate you, LOVE SPIRIT, and to give them the space also to live you, LOVE SPIRIT.

693. AS YOU ARE

Lord, I contemplate and adore you as you are, have been, and will be, unchanging and eternal.

694. SPIRITUAL WHOLENESS

Lord, most holy Spirit, I adore you as a unity, I adore you as a single whole, the same in character where-ever and whenever you are met, an unchanging Spirit being, today, tomorrow and for always. Praise be!

695. LORD, I AM SORRY (1)

Lord, I am sorry for my evil doings and not-doings; for my evil state, my evil spirit; for my follies, mistakes and insensitivities.
Lord, I am sorry. Have mercy upon me, have mercy upon me.

The following prayer evolved from 'Lord I am Sorry (1)'.

696. LORD, I AM SORRY (2)

Lord, I am sorry. Have mercy upon me, have mercy upon me.
Lord, I am sorry for my evil actions and my evil failures to act; I am sorry

for the evil spirit which resides within me, the consequence of my evil actions and my evil failures to act; and I am sorry for all that is wrong in your eyes in my life, for my stupidities, errors and insensitivities.

Lord, I am sorry. Have mercy upon me, have mercy upon me.

697. 2005 A YEAR OF LOVE

LORD, please assist me in this YEAR OF LOVE, OF LOVING, OF IMITATING YOUR LOVE; and in particular please help me in regard to loving myself, of acting for my good, and of pointing to you thereby.

698. TO BE ONE LOVING UNIT!

Come, Great Holy Spirit, who is alive in the present, as in the past and in the future, I give myself to you. Help me to serve you at all times, to be one serving unit!

Come, Great Holy Spirit, who is nearer than hands and feet, and in all that is excellent and admirable, I give myself to you. Help me to practise your Great Holy Spirit in all I do, to be one practising unit!

Come, Great Holy Spirit, who always speaks for the good of a person, whether in positive ideas or in restraints, I give myself to you. Help me to trust your utterances, to be one trusting unit!

Come, Great Holy Spirit, who is seen in the eternal verities, in truth, beauty and goodness, I give myself to you. Help me to manifest you in all places, to be one manifesting unit!

Come, Great Holy Spirit, who is about the business of love, I give myself to you. Help me to imitate your love, to be an instrument of your love, in relation to all, to be one loving unit!

699. SURELY NOT WEAPONS

Lord, I thank and praise you that your way is a way of love, and that being so surely it is better not to use weapons to achieve our goals, whether the weapons we use are physical, verbal or emotional. Lord, help us to use implements, words and feelings to serve your way, your way of love.

700. YOUR MOST HOLY SPIRIT - Y.M.H.S!
Lord God, please help me to submit to Y.M.H.S.,
to embody and to love Y.M.H.S.,
to live-out and to express Y.M.H.S.,
to point to Y.M.H.S. this day and forever more.

701. FOR LOVING KINDNESS
Lord, open my eyes, my heart, my pocket, my hands;
Lord, grant me the Spirit gift of loving-kindness.

702. FOR RETURNING
Almighty God, I thank and praise you for returning to your household, for belonging to you and your family, as did the prodigal son, as did Flo in Doreen Edward's novel, 'A Better Love Next Time'.

703. INVALUABLE THINGS
Almighty God, I thank and praise you for public worship, in particular the Meeting for Worship.
I thank and praise you for the gift of life. Help me to value and to appreciate it, and to show that I do so by living it properly and fully. So many murdered* people have not had the opportunity to do so.
And I thank and praise you for valuable groups, spiritual and cultural.
Lord, I thank and praise you for all good things.

*I was watching a series on Auschwitz at the time.

704. FOR WAITING
Spirit God, I thank and praise you for waiting, for waiting in lack of sight, in emptiness and in hopelessness. And I thank and praise you for waiting to be visited by love, in opportunities, in engaging ideas and in

further understanding. Holy Spirit, I thank and praise you for waiting.

705. THE ADORATION OF THE SPIRIT
Lord, I adore your Spirit, your most holy Spirit, a rare presence of love and beauty, enfolding, inspiring, assuring. Lord, I adore your most holy Spirit.

706. BY WHOSE LIGHT
Almighty God, I contemplate and adore you as a Holy Spirit, complete, pure and whole; as a Holy Spirit by whose light we are enabled to see the evil spirit we have within, the darkness in our beings. I praise and thank you for your Holy Spirit and for its light, and I am very sorry for my evil spirit.

707. FOUR 'UNs'
Lord, I contemplate and adore you as unconditional, unchanging and unending love. I seek to bring you a reflection of this in an undemanding love for all, for you, your children, including myself, and for your world. Praise be!

708. AS ONE WHO MATTERS
O Great, Eternal, Holy Spirit, I adore you as One who matters. I adore you as one who matters, an individual, human spirit. Lord, let there be no them and us between you and I, you, the Great, Eternal, Holy Spirit, and I the adoring, human spirit. And let there be no and them and us between human spirits at large, for this has been shown to be the great obscenity.

Any of the sentences of this prayer may be repeated as desired. The last sentence arose out of a Meeting for Worship, and again I think that the sentiment related to the Holocaust.

709. REGARDING LACK OF TRUST

Lord, I have shown great lack of trust in you and love of you. Help me to trust and love you, to trust your guidance and respect your Spirit activities in relation to me. Lord, help me to trust and love you.

710. TO CHANGE FOR THE BETTER

Lord, I am sorry for my sins and my sinfulness, for my wrongdoings and my wrong being in your sight. By the inspiration of your Holy Spirit please help me to change for the better.

711. INSIGHT

Almighty GOD, I thank and praise you for insight, for understanding, and for the insights which bring increased understanding. Grant that I may have insight and insights regarding all relationships and all activities. Praise be!

712. FOR THE PRESENCE

Lord God, I thank and praise you for the presence of your Spirit:
for it is by the light of your Spirit that I am enabled to see myself as I actually spiritually am; for it is by knowing that I am in the presence of your Spirit that I am enabled to properly evaluate my behaviour, to ask myself, is it suitable for such a privileged relationship; for it is by the coming forward of your Spirit that my mind is illuminated by inspirations and insights.
Lord God, I thank and praise you for the presence of your Spirit.

713. FOR THE CONSTANT PRESENCE

Almighty God, I thank and praise you for your constant presence, and for the fact that, as you see the need, you draw my attention to ideals, service me with good ideas, and support me in the ways in which I live; seek, by the opposition of the Spirit, to prevent me from behaving in erroneous ways; and protect me from people of ill will. Almighty God, I thank and praise you for your constant presence.

714. SPIRIT PROMPTS

Almighty God, I thank and praise you for your Words, for your Spirit prompts, in particular in relation to ...(specify) Help me to act appropriately in relation to your Words, to your Spirit prompts, and in particular those in relation to ...(specify)

And I thank you that on occasion you give me the assurance of your constant presence. Thank you, Lord.

715. TRUST

Almighty God, may I put you first in all matters, and to this end may I trust you in all matters.

716. THE GARMENTS OF YOUR NATURE

Lord, let me wear the garments of your nature: the hat of agape; the coat of caring; the belt of pointing to you; and the shoes of truth. Lord, let me wear the garments of your nature, today and everyday.

717. LOVE OF COMMUNITIES

Lord, help me to grow the well-being of the communities of which I am a member in love. Lord, help all who are members of these communities to grow their well-being in love.

718. MAKE LOVE

Lord, help me to make love with all, for all; make love in a relaxed, good-natured way.

719. THE POSSIBILITIES OF LIFE

Lord, give me the mind to see the possibilities of life, and the will to make some of these possibilities come to life. Yes, indeed!

Lemons

720. TO LOVE MY ENEMIES
Lord, help me to love my enemies, of which there are countless legions! However, all people are both friends and enemies, including myself!

721. TO KEEP ONSIDE
Almighty God, you are as you are in relation to your children, lovely and loving, whatever their character, body shape, clothes sense and conduct. May I remember this, and conduct myself in similar fashion in relation to your children, whatever their body shape and clothes sense, whatever their character and conduct. May I?

722. A RADIANCE OF YOUR SPIRIT
Lord, help me to be a setting-sun of your Spirit, and to remember that I am but half of the whole of any relationship, and that my hope is not to change, control or condemn anyone, but to love them, to be a radiance of your Spirit for them.

723. CRUCIFIXION
Lord, help me to accept all beings, yourself, other people, myself, and the necessity of crucifixion in these relationships, at any time, in any situation.

724. ALL OUR PARTS
Almighty God, I thank and praise you for our various body parts, and I pray that we may see each of them as enabling love, as enabling the well-being and continuity of the individual and the species, each and every one planned and evolved by you. Praise be!

725. ALLITERATIVE OBLATION
Most Holy Spirit, I give myself to you, tongue, teeth and toes.
I look for nothing for myself, as friendliness, fairness and favour,
but only to beam upon your world and its people your light, life and love,

to serve you as your advocate, ally and agent.
Most Holy Spirit, I give myself to you totally, Father, Liberty and Agape.

726. FOR A HEALTH PROBLEM
Lord, I hold-up to you my current health problem, which manifests itself in various ways, —-STATE—-. Lord, please assist those concerned in this problem in coming to a diagnosis of it. Given a correct diagnosis we shall know the way forward.

727. AS AMAZING GRACE
Lord, I adore you as amazing grace, amazing grace, amazing grace. Lord, I adore you.

728. AS TRUTH
Almighty God, I adore you as truth: the truth of the Holy Spiritual, the truth of the Holy Physical, the truth of Holy Reality.

729. RATTLED RATTLESNAKE
Heavenly Father, I contemplate and adore you as an ever-present, all-seeing, always pertinent God, ever ready to strike like a rattled rattlesnake with a Spirit input, with a word of love, always a friend. May I be ever ready to flee!

730. GLORIFIES (1)
Lord, I adore you as the One my being glorifies, my being glorifies, my being glorifies; Lord, I adore you as the One my existence glorifies, my existence glorifies, my existence glorifies.

731. GLORIFIES (2)
Lord, I adore you as the One my being of itself glorifies, glorifies,

glorifies; Lord, I adore you as the One my existence of itself glorifies, glorifies, glorifies. Praise be! Alleluia!

732. AS A BRILLIANCE
Almighty God, I adore you as a brilliance, as sparkling light imbued with love.
This phrase may be repeated as required.

733. TO ADORE THE LIVING GOD
Almighty God, I pray that you will reveal to me the way or ways in which you would have me adore you, which is to love you.

734. IMBUED WITH LOVE
Living God, I adore you as Light imbued with Love, as Spirit imbued with Love, as experiences of your Spirit imbued with love.

735. I ADORE YOU
Lord God, I adore you as Light! I adore you as Love! I adore you as Life! And I adore you for the experiences of your Spirit which have exemplified these: Light! Life! Love! Praise be!

736. GOD EXISTS
Lord, I adore you for the fact that you exist, I adore you for your existence. And I adore you for the fact that we are all your children, citizens in your kingdom, guests at your banquet, family members in your home. Lord, I adore you!

737. EVERYTHING
Lord, Most Holy Spirit, Divine One, I am sorry for everything about me which is wrong in your eyes. Lord, Most Holy Spirit, Divine One, I am

sorry, I feel sorry. Please forgive me for everything about me which is wrong in your eyes. I am happy to humble myself before you to say and be sorry for all that displeases you in me.

738. LORD, HEAR

Lord, hear my deepest longings; Lord, hear my highest aspirations; Lord, hear my widest desires; Lord, hear my prayer.
Adapted from a Sunday Link prayer (12.3.06).

739. FOR EVERYTHING

Lord, I am sorry for everything about me which is wrong, bad or evil in your eyes. I am sorry for crucifying you in the wrong, bad and evil things I think, say and do. Help me to love you and my neighbour - in loving my neighbour loving you - to be a force for agape, for the good of the recipients of our love.

740. TO BE A HILL

Love Spirit, I am sorry for my shortcomings, for my hardnesses of heart, for my unkindnesses of mind. By the power of your Love Spirit soften my heart, tune my mind.
May I be a hill filled with your Spirit, upon which your flora and fauna may grow and flourish, today and every day.

741. MY SINS AND SINFULNESS

Almighty God, I am sorry for my sins and sinfulness. I ask that you forgive me for my sins and sinfulness, and that you cleanse and heal me of their consequences.

742. CONSTANTLY PRESENT

Almighty God, I am sorry, I am very sorry, that I have not realised that your Spirit is constantly present to me, and that as a consequence I have

not ordered my behaviour appropriately for this state of affairs. Help me never to forget that your presence is in and around me at all times, and that therefore I should order my behaviour to be appropriate for this state of affairs. In this way whatever I am about I shall fulfill my calling, which is to point to you, today and every day.

743. LIFE IS FOR LIVING
Lord, I am sorry, I am sorry I have not recognised or valued the gift of life. Help me to recognise, accept and value the gift of life, and to live it in ways which are acceptable to you and myself. Help me not to deprive anyone else of such a precious gift, for example, by being party to a needless abortion, whether of a person or a relationship.

744. AS THE BUZZING FLY
Appropos the buzzing fly, Lord, help me to live-out my nature, which is an image of your nature, an image of your light, life and love.

745. TO YOUR ETERNAL REALITY
Almighty God, I thank and praise you for the opportunities we have to open our hearts and minds to your Eternal Reality, in Meetings for Worship, private devotions and when disengaged from activities, as during the night. And I thank and praise you for the illuminations which you grant to us, perhaps as a result of our opening our hearts and minds to your Eternal Reality. I thank and praise you for your Eternal Reality, and the light which it bestows upon us.

746. FOR THE LANDSCAPE
Love Spirit, I thank and praise you for your landscape: for the skies, the fields, the hedgerows and the trees; for the farmhouse and the farm, the hare and the skylark; for the farmer turning hay; for the farmer on the next occasion coming to check me out and chatting with me; for myself drawing in the sunshine and the cloud shadow.

Love Spirit, I thank and praise you for your landscape.

747. FOR THE CONSTANT PRESENCE OF THE LORD
Lord, I thank and praise you that I live in your presence, that you are always with me, and I thank and praise you for the occasions when I remember that this is so.

748. A PRAYER FOR CLEANSING
Lord, send your Spirit to me and bless me;
Lord, send your Spirit to me and cleanse and heal me;
Lord, in your Spirit say, 'Be silent and come out of him!'

749. MAY WE GROW TOGETHER
Lord, help us to show generosity of spirit and respect to others, whatever their religious, political and social affiliations may be. May we grow together in your Truth this day and forever more.

750. PROBLEMS
Almighty God, I pray that you will teach me how to handle problems, problems in relation to others, whether individuals or bodies, and problems in relation to myself.

751. RIGHT ON THE NAIL
Almighty God, I thank and praise you for being right on the nail! Help me to recognise your word, to appreciate and to trust it; and help me to act appropriately in the situation then obtaining in response to your utterance, it being right on the nail!

752. FOR THE FORGETFUL
The following prayer is for those who are forgetful with respect to remembering people's names. Generally we can find a work-around, but

sometimes when we have known a person for a long time we might feel we should be doing better.

Almighty God, I pray that I may try harder to remember people's names, in particular that of ...NAME... I ask your blessings upon ...HIM/HER..., the blessings of your love, both directly and angelically, in the present and in the future; and I ask this for everyone.

753. YOUR KINGDOM, YOUR BANQUET, YOUR HOME

Lord, the world is your kingdom, your banquet, your home, and I praise and thank you that this is so. Everyone, whether they know it or not, is a citizen of your kingdom, a guest at your banquet, a family member in your home! And so, with your ever-ready help, I give my unconditional, undying love and respect to everyone, fellow citizen, fellow guest, fellow family member!

754. DEPRESSION

Lord, may I wash your feet and the feet of your children with my tears, with my depressed condition, with my unasked for being, my unasked for existence.

755. UNIQUE

Lord, I thank and praise you for the uniqueness of your children. Help me to love and to appreciate them in their uniqueness: the uniqueness of their personalities, their souls, the uniqueness of their experience of you, and the uniqueness of their experience of life, which has had its downs as well as its ups. Lord, I thank and praise you for the uniqueness of your children.

756. HUMANITY

Lord, I pray that you will enable me to accept and respect the manifold biological complexities of our humanity, for they are necessary for our individual existences and our survival as a species. Lord, I pray that you will enable me to accept our humanity.

757. THE LIGHT OF CONSCIOUSNESS
Almighty God, I thank and praise you for Light, and in particular the light of consciousness. May our light of consciousness, by which we live, be imbued with love, with holy love, with holy kindliness.

758. MADE IN YOUR IMAGE
Almighty God, I thank and praise you for the images we have of you, one of which is that you are Spirit, expressing your Spirit in light, life and love. And I thank and praise you that we reflect your image, for example, we have the light of consciousness, the life of being alive, and the love of having the biological machinery which enables our being alive and our offspring.

759. THE PRAYER OF AN ASPIRANT ANGEL
Lord, I aim to promote the good, that which is beneficial, and improve the bad, that which is harmful; and I seek your support in the rational pursuit of these aims as an aspirant angel!

760. MORNING ADORATION
Living God, I adore you for your creation:
for the newly risen sun, shining brightly and bringing lovely colour to the morning clouds;
for the early morning mist, through which the sun can appear as a white orb;
and for the light snowfall, covering the fields, but with green showing here and there.
For all these things, Lord, I adore you.

761. SUPPORTIVE
Lord, I adore you for being supportive in evolutionary terms, for thinking of everything, for example, the continuation of the species; Lord, I adore you for being supportive in the present, always understanding, at all times you do your best; and I adore you for being supportive in the future, for your nature remains the same. Alleluia!

762. TO YOUR GLORY
Lord, that which is good in me, in my conduct and in my activities, I offer up to your glory, for your glory. Alleluia!

763. I PRAISE YOU (1)
Eternal Being, I praise you with my words;
Eternal Being, I praise you with my living;
Eternal Being, I praise you with my dying.
Eternal Being, let every part of me, every moment of me, praise you!

764. I PRAISE YOU (2)
Eternal Being, I praise you with my words:
my words of love scattered for all; my words of enlightenment broadcast for all, my words of life sown for all.
Eternal Being, I praise you with my acts:
my acts of living scattered for all; my acts of illumination broadcast for all; my acts of creation sown for all. Praise be!

765. MAY I PRAISE YOU
Eternal Being, may I praise you with my dying:
may my dying promote and point to you for all;
may my dying be for the good of all;
and may my dying be a preparation for a new life, and an entry into it. Praise be!

766.   HOLY GOD, I PRAISE YOU
Holy God, I praise you with *my writing and my picture-making; Holy God, I praise you with *my visiting and my S.P.U.C. activities. Holy God, let all that I say or do praise you! Praise you!

*Replace activities as appropriate.

767.   INTELLIGENCE
Heavenly Father, I adore you for your intelligence, your vast intelligence, your unbelievably great intelligence; I adore you for your foresight, your tremendous foresight, your unbelievably magnificent foresight; and I adore you for the expression of your intelligence and foresight in your created order, your astounding created order, your unbelievably amazing created order. Praise be!

768.   When undertaking an activity or relationship, whether new or continuing, it can be held up to God. This would seem good, sensible practice.

FOR MY ADORATION
Living God, I hold upto you my adoration for the coming week. I ask that you will guide and inspire my adoration that it might be pleasing to you.

769.   FOR LIGHT
Heavenly Father, I adore you for the wonder of physical light, its rays flying through and about the universe at enormous speed, granting us the illumination of all that we see. Heavenly Father, I adore you for light, for physical light. And I adore you also for spiritual light, again all pervasive, engaging with the human psyche and granting us inspiration, guidance and insight. Heavenly Father, I adore you for the wonder of

light, both physical and spiritual.

770. AS YOU ARE
Heavenly Father, Eternal Being, I adore you as you are.

771. A PENITENCE
Lord, I am sorry for my sins and for my sinfulness, for the doings I have done and the being which I have been, which have been against you, your nature and your purposes.

772. HORRIBLE, VILE
Lord, may I eschew horrible thoughts and language, vile thoughts and language.

773. FOR PURITY OF HEART
Lord, by the power of your Spirit, make my heart clean, my mind clean, my body clean, my spirit clean, and fit for purpose, Lord, your purposes. To this end I shall try to eschew bad language, whether in my head or in my mouth. Praise be to you, O Lord.

774. POVERTY OF SPIRIT
Lord, may I put your love first, your love before what I think others may think, and to this end may I espouse love of you and poverty of spirit, go with the flow of your Spirit.

775. IRRESPONSIVE
Lord, I am sorry for my wrongdoings, in particular not taking on board your Spirit utterances, for being irresponsive in relation to them; for putting fear of the outlook of your children, whether real or imagined, above your outlook in any given matter. Lord, help me to hear, to think

about and respond sensibly to the things of your Spirit, to the words of your Spirit, today and always.

776.   A DEPRESSIVE'S PRAYER
I am sorry that I exist. (3x) Lord, have mercy upon me. (3x)

777.   NOT AS I SHOULD BE
Heavenly King, I am sorry that I am not the person you would have me to be, the person you have in your mind's eye. Help me, please, to become that person, in this life especially.

778.   ALLELUIA! AGAPE!
Living God, I thank and praise you for Alleluia, for the possibility and opportunities to praise you, to adore you, to contemplate you; and I praise and thank you for Agape, for the possibility and opportunities to love your children, to care for them, to be compassionate in respect to them. Praise be!

779.   FOR PHYSICAL LIGHT
Heavenly Being, I thank and praise you for physical light, the light which illumines your world, revealing to us scenic attraction, beautiful colour, shape and form, and endless miracle; I thank and praise you for sources of light, the sun and moon, and lamps of every kind; and I thank and praise you for our senses, in particular our eyes, which enable our appreciation, knowledge and enjoyment of your world. Praise be!

780.   FOR SPIRIT UTTERANCES
Heavenly Father, I thank and praise you for Your Spirit utterances: those taking a visual form; those which manifest themselves in fundamental ideas; those providingthe aroma of a loving suggestion; those which strongly weigh against a proposed course of conduct or action; and those

which show the way forward in a relationship or activity. Lord, I thank and praise you for your Spirit utterances in all their incredible variety, in whatever ways they are expressed. Thanks be!

781.　FOR FRIENDSHIP

Heavenly Father, I thank and praise you for friendship, for friendship with other people, for example ———, but also for friendship with You and with myself. Help me to try to grow friendship with others, not forgetting my family, Yourself and myself, which is most important. By attempting to be a friend I bring myself in line with You, Spirit, Power and Presence. Thanks and praise be to You!

782.　FOR HELPFUL INPUTS

Heavenly Father, I thank and praise you for helpful inputs: for helpful inputs from your children, such as constructive suggestions and appreciative comments; for helpful inputs from yourself, unexpected and surprising though they are; for helpful inputs from your creation, both physical and spiritual, such as a fine sunrise; and helpful inputs from myself, as in daily maintenance.

Grant that I may love and respect you, your creation, your children and myself this day and forevermore. Heavenly Father, I thank and praise you for helpful inputs.

783.　BE LOVE, DO LOVE

Heavenly Father, I thank and praise you for the two great commandments and for their importance in our lives; and I thank and praise you for our multifaceted physical beings and our many abilities, making both our living and our loving possible and doable. I thank and praise you!

784.　TRUST, ACCEPTANCE AND PRIORITY

Living God, I come before you in love, and pray that I may give you, as aspects of my love for you, trust, acceptance and priority. May I recognise that you know better than I do and seek, not forgoing personal integrity in any way, to take your Spirit utterances on board. This is not easy, given that you operate at a different, somewhat higher level than I do! Also, may I try to give you priority over the actual and supposed views of others. May I try to give you trust, acceptance and priority!

785.   The following prayer is for the sports team (or teams) you support. Insert such names as are appropriate:
FOR ....
Living God, I pray for ....:
for the chairperson, ..., and for the board; for the head coach, ..., and his management team; for the players at whichever level; for all the ancillary staff, such as the ground staff and stewards; and for the supporters, includingg their fans' groups. Grant your grace and graciousness upon all those involved with .... in any way, shape or form.

786.   LORD, SHOW ME THE WAY FORWARD
Lord, show me the way forward in respect to: the use I put my life for you; the work I do for you; having a partner; and my disposition of Sundays. Lord, show me the way forward!

787.   FOR THE EARLY MORNING SUN
Holy God, I thank and praise you for the rising sun, and the beautiful cloud colours spreading outwards;
I thank and praise you for morning mist and the white orb shining through;
and I thank and praise you for the light and warmth of which this daily miracle is a herald!
Holy God, I thank and praise you!

Winster Street

788.   THE IMPERFECT
Lord, it is not the perfect, but the imperfect, who have need of love.*
Your love and your love in human love can together bring to the
imperfect enrichment and fulfillment. Grant us relationships and activities
which will help to enable these things. Thank you, Lord.

*Oscar Wilde.

789.   FRIENDSHIP
Lord, may I seek to grow friendship with all, female and male, young and
old, with yourself, with myself. And may some at least seek to grow
friendship with me.

790.   FOR NOT RECOGNISING THE SPIRIT
I acknowledge that I have not understood the activity of the Spirit in
relation to me, nor have I responded to it appropriately, picked-up on it
as I could have done. I am sorry, have mercy upon me.

791.   A PURE LOVE FOR ALL
Lord, grant me a pure love for all, for yourself, for your children and for
your world, both animate and inanimate. Thankyou, Lord.

792.   A PURE LOVE FOR ALL FOREVER
Lord, grant me a pure love for all forever. From now on may I be
committed to loving everyone and everything. Lord, grant me a pure
love for all. forever, thus imitating and being instrumental of your eternal
love. Thankyou, Lord.

793.   EVER PRESENT
Lord, help me to be open to the Holy Spirit, whatever activity I am
engaged in. Help me to be a wise virgin, with the oil of receptivity in my

lamp at all times, rather than a foolish one, unaware that the Spirit is ever present and may speak at any time.

794. FOR THE DIVINE LOVELINESS
Heavenly King, I adore you as you are; I adore you in your divine loveliness. [Repeated as required.]

795. SPEAKS IN LOVE
Lord, I adore you as the One who speaks in love, who speaks to guide and support those you address. Help us to recognise this, and to respond appropriately to your utterances.

796. FOR YOUR LOVE
Lord, I adore you for your love; help me to live in your love and to do so sensibly and effectively. Yes, Lord!

797. AS ONE WHO WASHES FEET
Heavenly Being, I adore you.
I adore you as one who washes feet, as one who comes to us to serve; I adore you as one who speaks in love, as one who comes to us to uphold; and I adore you as one who opposes that which harms, who comes to us to protect.
Heavenly Being, I adore you.

798. LIFE'S CENTRE
Heavenly Father and Mother, I adore and praise you for revealing what, in your eyes, my life is about, that I am and live in relationship to your Most Holy Spirit. I praise you for this relationship, and for the possibility of embodying your Most Holy Spirit, and the opportunities to show and express its qualities, its fruits. Heavenly Father and Mother, I adore and praise you for my relationship to you.

799.   INFINITE REALITY
Infinite Reality, I adore and praise you!
I adore and praise you for Sister Spirit, her guidance and upholding;
I adore and praise you for Brother Sun, his shine and warming;
I adore and praise you for Sister Light, her lightness of touch and revealing;
and I adore and praise you for Brother Water, his coolness and refreshing.
Infinite Reality, I adore and praise you for the multitudinous miracles we inhabit day by day, hour by hour. Praise be!

800.   LOOKING AND UNDERSTANDING
Heavenly Tutor, I pray that I may look hard at and understand well what is in front of me, that I may abide by its basic proportions, and that I may not feel overwhelmed by what is there, but rather patiently tease-out the visual information, with pen, pencil or brush.

801.   FOR THE BEAUTY
Heavenly Creator, I adore, praise and thank you for the BEAUTY of your creation, of the world in which we live.

802.   ALWAYS PRESENT, ALWAYS LOVE
Heavenly Light, I adore and praise you as the one who is always present, whose address, whether positive or oppositional, is always for our good, who always brings love to the table.

803.   THE GIFT OF LIFE
Heavenly Father and Mother, I adore and praise you for the gift of life, made possible by a vast universe and a vast time-scale. May I enjoy my gift.
May I enjoy my gift in doing my best to live love in the present for all.
May I enjoy my gift in contentment in modest doings and achievements.

May I enjoy my gift, which I ak in your name, Heavenly Father and Mother.

804. FOR EXISTING
Heavenly Reality, I adore and praise you for existing, for existing throughout space and time, and for existing in a personal relationship with each and every one of us.

805. NOT HURTING, BUT GROWING
Heavenly Father, I am sorry for those times I have hurt or harmed a person, or a community, whether wittingly or unwittingly. And I am sorry for those times I have not grown things in love, have not grown relationships in love, or activities. Help me to recognise that such growing is supported by the power and illumination of the Spirit and that the things thus grown are 'love your neighbour' things; that such growing is done in a rational way; and that making mistakes and things going wrong are always a part of it.

806. TO DO BETTER (1)
Lord, I am sorry for my sins and my sinfulness. Please help me to do better in the things in which you think I should do better in respect to the different centres of my being. Help me to bring agape to them all! Yes, Lord!

807. RESPONSIBILITY
Living God, while it is true that my coming into existence was outside of my control, I recognise that I am responsible for my attitude to, and use of, my existence. May this recognition increase.

808. TO DO BETTER (2)
Loving God, I am sorry for my wrongdoings and my wrongbeing. Please help me to do better in the things in in which you think I can do better. Bring them to my attention, and promote knowledge and insights which

will provide the understanding to enable me to make improvements. Loving God, I ask this in the name of Love.

809.   I AM SORRY

I am sorry for those times when I have hurt or harmed any person in any way, shape or form, whether wittingly or inadvertently. Have mercy, have mercy upon me, and please forgive me.
With the aid of your most holy Spirit may I desist from such conduct in the future, may I desist from hurting or harming you, my neighbour and myself. Have mercy, have mercy upon me.

810.   TO LABOUR

Most Holy Spirit, help me to bless both others and myself, to appreciate beauty in its various forms, and to labour for the goals I have, to love, to pray and to point to you. I am sorry for my imperfection and the imperfect things I think say and do.

811.   WHEN DEPRESSED

Heavenly Parent, I come before you in apology for my depressed condition, for my failure in all aspects of my life, for grumbling - for being a Mr Grump, and for not being responsive to your Spirit's expressions of love, for not trusting you. Heavenly Parent, have mercy, Divine Reality, have mercy, Heavenly Parent, have mercy.

812.   FOR SELF RELIANCE

I Heavenly Parent, may I trust you, but may I also trust my loving, thinking and doing. May I aspire to be self-reliant.

II Heavenly Power, may I rest in self-reliance in respect to being love and doing love, in respect to upholding truth and expressing truth, and in respect to being good and good conduct. Heavenly Power, may I value self-reliance.

III Heavenly Spirit, may I rest self-reliantly in love, in the fact of the matter and in being creative.

813. TO IMPROVE

Heavenly Father and Mother, I am sorry for having been and for being stupid. Help me rather to try to be intelligent, sensible, on the ball. I am sorry for having been and for being ignorant. Help me to make myself informed in personal and important matters. And I am sorry for having been and being careless with respect to the prompting of my conscience. Help me rather to be guided by it. Heavenly Father and Mother, I ask these things in your name.

814. IMPERFECT

Father and Mother, I am sorry for not seeing that I must seek the goals I have in the context of imperfection. May I struggle to do better at all times.

815. FOR THE GIFT OF LIFE

Heavenly Father, I thank and praise you for the gift of life, and for all aspects of our psyches and physiques: for our spirits, which by your Spirit can be cleansed, healed and made whole; for the many evolved, biological systems we embody, and which make life possible; and for the fact that we can know you experimentally. Heavenly Father, I thank and praise you for the gift of life!

816. FOR THE GIFT OF LIFE (2)

Heavenly Father, I thank and praise you for the gift of life: for our digestive and reproductive systems as aspects of this gift, and for brains in reasonable order. Praise be!

817. ALL PEOPLE, ALL COMMUNITIES
Divine Reality, I thank and praise you for all people and all communities, in particular those with whom I reside, those with whom I worship, those with whom I work, and those with whom I pursue my interests. I pray that I may love, value and serve each and every one of them.

818. IN PARTICULAR
Mother and Father, I thank you for food and drink, in particular that I have enough of both; I thank you for light, and for lights, in particular for candles; I thank you for company, in particular that I receive when visiting; and I thank you for flowers, in particular for flag and for foxglove. Mother and Father, I thank you for all good things.

819. AN INTEGRAL PART
I thank and praise you for desire, an integral part of the reproductive process by which new humans, new souls, are brought into being; I thank and praise you for the cup that cheers, an integral part of arising from bed by which new days, new nights, are brought into being; and I thank and praise you for drawing and painting, an integral part of showing appreciation of you and your world and by which new pictures are brought into being. Heavenly Father and Mother, I thank and praise you for these and all good things.

820. WHICH MAY BE SEEN
Heavenly Father and Mother, I thank you for the sharp darts of your love, which may be seen in your leadings and oppositions; I thank you for the gift of life, which may be seen as a lovely thing, as a pure bonus; and I thank you for obtaining the knowledge which dispels our ignorance. Heavenly Father and Mother, I thank you for these things.

821. JESUS AS A GIFT
O Spirit, I thank and praise you for our brother, Jesus, whose teachings

have had such a widespread influence and in particular upon myself, and I thank and praise you for all our brothers and sisters, each your child, each making their contributions to their families and communities. Praise be!

822. THE WAY FORWARD

Heavenly Father, please cleanse and heal me of all the evil within me and make me whole; please advise me regarding the work I do – what work I do and how I do it; and please help me to take fully on board the promptings and upholdings of light and life and love, and at the same time make rational decisions about what I am to do in connexion with any given matter.

823. THE RIGHT KIND OF HELP

Lord, I pray that you will give me the right kind of help and support, not only in respect to my activities, although this is much appreciated, but also in respect to my relationship, in particular girlfriends★, potential or actual.

★or boyfriends!

824. CURRENT ILLNESS

Lord, I hold up to you the current illness I have with regard to ...
(If required: I also hold up to you ...)

825. ANY GIRLFRIEND (Adapt for BOY)

Lord, I hold in your light, life and love any future girlfriend I may have. I pray that she may live in your light, life and love in me. May my heart be warm, sensitive and loving, my mind reasonable, rational and responsible, and may I never forget that all relationships are love relationships. Praise be!

826.   WHOSE I AM
Lord, help me to remember whose I am. May I live responsibly before you, and may I never betray you because I am worried about what a person thinks. You are the centre of all my human centres, whether you support or oppose, at all times and in all places, situations and relationships. Yes, Lord!

827.   DO UNTO GOD
Divine Reality, I pray that I may do unto you as I hope you will do unto me. Yes, O Heavenly One!

828.   DO UNTO GOD AS GOD DOES UNTO YOU
Strange, Strong Spirit, I pray that I may conduct myself towards you as you conduct yourself towards me, purposefully, positively, protectively, profoundly. Heavenly Strength, I thankyou.

829.   TO TRUST
Heavenly Parent, I pray that you will help me to register and to trust the expressions of your Spirit in my heart and mind.

830.   TO BE CONTENT
Heavenly Love, help me to be content in being a good spirit, shading, perhaps, into being a God Spirit, and content also in being of use both to others and to myself.

831.   RESOLVING PROBLEMS
Heavenly Father, I pray that I may see resolving problems as an aspect of love, and that when I try to resolve a problem I may do so with consideration and courtesy. Help me to avoid hostility and hatred, but rather keep in the forefront of my mind the good of the person or persons with whom I am trying to resolve the problem, and indeed the

good of the communities to which I belong. May I keep in the forefront of my mind the good of every person with whom I share life's path.

832. OUR LOVES
Heavenly Father and Mother, help me to remember that your love, my girlfriend's love and my own are always present in our relationships, are always present at the table. Help me to go forward in these different loves.

833. MAKING DECISIONS
Living God, help me to remember to come before you when making important decisions, and to invite your guidance and wisdom in making them.

834. THIS DAY
I Help me this day, O Spirit, to do my best in my conduct and in my activities, and thus glorify you, wondrous Power, wondrous Being.

II Raise me this day, O Spirit, above all that is mean and lowly, and thus uphold you, wondrous Power, wondrous Being.

III Remind me this day, O Spirit, to make decisions based on love, the good of persons, and thus imitate you, wondrous Power, wondrous Being.

835. AN AFFIRMATION
The Light and Love of God reach over all, the Light and Love of God seek the good of all; the Light and Love of God in me reach over all, the Light and Love of God in me seek the good of all; and I try to see that my light and love reach over all, that my light and love seek the good of all, in imitation of and in harmony with the Light and Love of God, which reach over all, which seek the good of all.

836.   ABSOLUTELY
Heavenly Power, I pray that I may be your Agape for all at all times, that is, absolutely; that I may aim to point to you whatever I am being and doing, that is, absolutely; and that I may seek appropriate goods in all circumstances, that is, absolutely. Help me to be mindful of these goals today and every day, and in doing so fulfill your purposes for me, to an extent, if not absolutely!

837.   FOR THE GOOD OF
Heavenly Father and Mother, I pray that I may find well-being, purpose and personal fulfillment in my life today. May what I say think and do harmonise with your glory, and be for the good of your children and your world.

838.   GOOD THINGS
Divine Reality, I pray that you will uphold those things in our lives which you see as good; oppose those things which you see as bad; and open to us those things which are good and which you would have us pursue, but which are currently absent from our lives.

839.   SEXUAL CAPABILITIES
Divine Reality, I pray that you will show us what in your eyes are the right and proper expressions of our sexual capabilities, what are the good things you would have us pursue in respect to them.

840.   BRING GOOD INTO BEING
O Good Being, I pray that I may see all my various activities as love activities, that is, as activities which bring goods, material and spiritual, into being, goods which point to you, a Good Being, a God Being.

841. CO-WORKER

Heavenly Father and Mother, I pray that I may bring goods into being. By doing so I may bring your divine love into being, bring Agape into being, and fulfill the Two Great Commandments. By doing so I may be a co-worker with you, the source of all goods, all true goods.

842. AM I HEARD? HAVE I BEEN HEARD?

O Summum Bonum! O Summum Bonum! Am I heard? Have I been heard? Hearing a person is a good and must be contained in you, the embodiment of all goods, O Summum Bonum, O Summum Bonum. Yes, I am heard! Yes, I have been heard!

Have I been responded to? Yes, I have been responded to, and always for my good! Not surprisingly, however, I have not necessarily understood your responses, and so have not been in a position to implement them, to take advantage of them. I have not acted on your responses, they have gone by the board and life has moved on. In certain instances this has proved to be heart-breaking, life-breaking.

Life at large is self-ordering and I can remember this. I could also try to be much more careful with my decisions; and with respect to your responses I could try harder to get my head round them and to implement them positively. It will help me to remember that you love me, and this being the case that I can trust you, O Summum Bonum, O Summum Bonum!

843. TO BE

Gracious God, I pray that we may attempt to be pure love, pure light and pure life for all at all times. Gracious God, I pray that we may attempt to be these things.

844. A PRAYER FOR VISION

Heavenly Father and Mother, I pray that you will grant me this vision that you would have me have, and to know the particular ways in which I might work to share that vision.

845. MY WRONG BEINGS AND DOINGS
I am sorry for my wrong being and my recent wrong doings. I pray that by the shining of your light you will expose that which is wrong in my inner being, and that which is wrong regarding my conduct and my activities, and reveal to me how I might bring about improvements in respect to these, my innner being, my conduct and my activities.

846. VALUING ALL (1)
O Supreme Atman, I am sorry I have not valued others, or indeed myself, as I should have done, have not seen that we are souls of infinite worth. Have mercy upon me.

847. VALUING ALL (2)
Heavenly Parent, I am sorry that I have not seen people as human beings having immeasurable intrinsic value, whatever our appearance, our colour, size and shape, our religion and our social and economic status. Have mercy upon me. I am sorry that I have not valued others, and indeed myself, as I should have done.

848. FOR BEING A SNOB
Great Spirit, I am sorry for being a snob, for being distanced from my fellow human beings by their physical appearance, and their social and economic status. Help me to give full acceptance to a person, and to do so because I recognise their value, rather than because I wish them to behave in particular ways towards me.

849. WITHOUT APPRECIATION, WITHOUT LOVE
Heavenly Parent, I am sorry for not having appreciated and enjoyed the gift of life as well as I might have done. Also, I am sorry for not having loved in and through all that I do. Help me to appreciate my gift of life

better, and to love my garden and gardening in it, bringing on therein good things for myself and for others, thereby pointing to you, the God of good things.3

850. FOR SPRINGTIME WEATHER

Heavenly Father and Mother, I thank, praise and adore you for the sunny weather we are enjoying this week. I love the clarity and the colour it brings to our streets and our landscapes. Heavenly Father and Mother, I thank, praise and adore you for the sunny, fresh weather.

851. FOR CLIMATE, FLORA AND FAUNA

Heavenly Parent, I thank, praise and adore you for the temperate climate of the British Isles, for the beautiful flora to which it gives rise, and for the variety of fauna with its many birds and mammals, for example, otters and beavers.

852. FOR COMPANY

Heavenly Parent, I thank, praise and adore you for company, and in particular the company provided by art★ groups.
★as appropriate

853. FOR VALUING A PERSON

Heavenly Parent, I thank, praise and adore you for the new physical things I have, my new windows, curtains and nets; and also for the intangible things, such as love, respect and valuing a person. Heavenly Parent, I thank, praise and adore you for these things.

854. FOR THE GIFT OF LIFE

O Great Spirit, I thank, praise and adore you for the gift of life. I pray that I may try to value it and to put it to good use. Some have it cruelly taken from them. Help me to appreciate and enjoy what I continue to have, the gift of life.

855.   FOR MODERN DENTISTRY
Most Holy Spirit, I thank, praise and adore you for modern dentistry, that oral problems may be addressed, usually safely and relatively painlessly.

856.   OUR AMAZING UNIVERSE
Divine Reality, I am thankful, I am grateful, for the experience I have had of an amazing universe, such a huge design, such a complex design, spatially and temporally; and I am thankful, I am grateful, for the dedication of those who have enabled our vision and understanding of the greater and smaller universes. Divine Reality, I am thankful, I am grateful.

857.   FOR AN INDIAN SUMMER
Heavenly Parent, I thank, praise and adore you for the Indian summer we are currently enjoying, the mellow warmth of the sun, the brisk coolness of the anticipatory breezes, the softness of the skyscapes, the beauty of autumnal gardens, both English and Japanese, where your life-force burgeons up in a multitudinous variety of forms, manifesting beauty, all to the glory of your power, your hidden mysterious power, invisible, immaterial and immanent.
A girl, replacing starfish in the sea, was asked why she did it, when there were so many on the beach. She said it mattered to those she did rescue.

858.   GOOD FOR SOMEONE
Great Being, I thank and praise you for this story and for the opportunities we have to be helpful, if not to everyone, then at least to a few.

859.   FOR OUR CREATIVE GIFTS
Great Being, I adore, praise and thank you for our creative gifts, such as art and music. They give us sensible and absorbing occupation of our time, with, possibly, positive outcomes for ourselves and others; and I

thank you that by them we can become co-creators, and point to you and your miraculous world. Great Being!

860.　DAWN 1
Great Creator, I thank and praise you for early morning skies, the subtle colour, the gentle illumination of silhouetted forms, the growing radiance, becoming so strong I dare not look for long, the shadow sides of clouds a subdued grey. Great Creator, I thank and praise you for early morning skies.

861.　DAWN 2
Great Creator, I thank and praise you for this dawn, the brightening cerulean blue, the high, illumined, grey-orange cloud, and below the fast moving, wind blown, dark grey racers. Great Creator, I thank and praise you for skies, and in particular this morning's dawn.

862.　THIS VERY DAY
Great Spirit, I thank you for the opportunity to be a blessing this very day, that is, a channel through which your love can flow for all. I thank and praise you for this, and that such an opportunity can give meaning, can give point and purpose, to this particular day. Praise be!

863.　GRACE AND TRUTH
Heavenly Father and Mother, I pray that I may be an active steward of your grace and truth, an effective vehicle of your grace and truth, in relation to you, all your children and your world.

864.　THE SEA AT HUNSTANTON
I. Heavenly Parent, I thank, praise and adore you for the relationship between the colours of the sea and the sun and cloud overhead.
II. Heavenly Parent, I thank, praise and adore you for the lovely cloudscapes on the Norfolk coast and the effect they have upon the

colours and tones of the sea.

865. BY MY CONDUCT
Most Holy Spirit, I pray that I may conduct myself with love, respect and trust in relation to you, experiences of the Spirit, other people, myself and the physical world; and that by my conduct I may give my testimony, witness to you, point to you.

866. GOOD CONDUCT, GOOD WORKS!
Heavenly Parent, I pray that I may point to you, both by how I conduct myself, and by seeking to bring good things, good works, into everyone's life, not forgetting your own.

867. TO DO WHAT I DO WELL
Great Creator, I pray that I may do whatever I do well, whether it be praying, conversing, or other activity. May what I do, what I produce, be good as I understand good in regard to the particular activity, but may it also be good in your eyes. I pray that I may do whatever I do with care and patience.

868. TEACH ME
O Divine Reality, teach me how you would have me pray; teach me how you would have me point to you; teach me how you would have me love in my dwelling place; teach me, O Divine Reality, the things pertinent to the living of my life, as you would have me live it.

869. ALL PEOPLE MATTER
Heavenly Father and Mother, we affirm that you love your children, and it is true that in a miraculous world there are infinite positives, and yet it is also true that there are terrible negatives, such as diseases and disasters. Even that which we see as a great gift, free will, can lead to our great hurt, when we use it mistakenly through ignorance and other deficiencies.

Our mistakes can lead to life-long deprivation rather than fulness of life. Given that you speak to us through the things in the world we ask that you will help us to be guided and inspired by what we see, hear and read, by what we experience; and we ask also that you will speak directly to us in helping to bring us fuller and happier lives.

870. FOR ALL
Lady, Lord, help me to pursue love for all, kindness for all, loving-kindness for all; help me to be an agape human being for all.

871. FOR SLEEP
Pertinent Spirit, I thank and praise you for the gift of sleep, such a lovely gift! Grow my appreciation of sleep, and help me to order it in such ways that it makes an optimal contribution to my work for the people of your amazing world. Let my works be jewels, if little ones!

872. TO BE A BLESSING
Lord, help me to be a blessing in all that I am, and to bless in all that I think, say and do.

873. TO NURTURE THE GOOD IN ME
Heavenly Father and Mother, I pray that by the power of your Spirit you will nurture in me that which is good in your eyes.

874. TO SHAPE AND INFLUENCE
Heavenly Father and Mother, I pray that in my public and private worship you will shape and influence my heart, mind and soul.

875. THE BASIC, REGULAR REQUESTS
Heavenly Father and Mother, I pray that you will grant these requests:

Here the person praying lists those requests which he/she feels merit being regularly brought before the Divine Reality. An 'x' request can be included, where 'x' equals those things which the Divine thinks we should be praying for but are not.

876.   FOR THE DAY
Heavenly Parent, I hold-up to you this particular day, and pray that I may utilise it in the ways which are optimal in respect to your purposes and love.

877.   ALL THINGS!
Heavenly Parent, I pray for those things for which I regularly do pray, and also anything which you think I should pray for, but presently do not. Illumine me!

878.   TO BE AND TO DO
Most Holy Spirit, I pray that you will help me to be like the sun, to be light and warmth and to do light and warmth; to be like a mother, to be love and loving and to do love and loving; and to be like a good rabbi, to be blessings and to do blessings.
Pam Ayres alludes to maternal love in 'The Akaroa Cannon', while the rabbi I had in mind was Rabbi Lionel Blue.

879.   TO BE AND DO GOOD
Heavenly Spirit, I pray that I may be good and do good, and thereby be an apprentice, agape angel.

880.   HAVE A NICE DAY!
Ever Present One, may I have a nice day! May I today add to the good things of life rather than the bad, the love things of life rather than the hating. Ever Present One, hear my prayer.

In the prayer following I used the definition of 'nice' found in the Little Oxford Dictionary.

881.   HAVE A NICE DAY! (2)

Heavenly Being, I pray that I may have an agreeable day, and that I may be kind, friendly and considerate, and in my activities subtle, fine and fastidious. Heavenly Being, hear my prayer I beseech you.

Signpost, Willoughby

ISBN 978-1848765-320